THOUGHTS ON THE TIMES AND SEASONS

OF

SACRED PROPHECY.

BY

THOMAS RAWSON BIRKS, M.A.,

Knightbridge Professor of Moral Philosophy and Theology in the University of Cambridge; and late Vicar of Holy Trinity, Cambridge.

WITH A PREFACE

BY

EDWARD BICKERSTETH BIRKS, M.A.,

FELLOW OF TRINITY COLLEGE, CAMBRIDGE.

𝔏𝔬𝔫𝔡𝔬𝔫 :

HODDER AND STOUGHTON,

27, PATERNOSTER ROW.

—

MDCCCLXXX.

PREFACE.

THIS little book consists of four parts. The author had often been urged to republish some of his early works on prophecy, but had never found the leisure requisite. Suddenly he discovered that in the fifth edition of the late Mr. Elliott's *Horæ Apocalypticæ*, he was credited with a conversion to notions to which he had never been converted, and that this misrepresentation of his views, founded on a misapprehension of his meaning in a private letter, had long been in circulation, while he himself had been left wholly uninformed of it; and he felt it his duty to protest. It seemed that the error might most simply be corrected by reprinting his earliest utterances on the structure of the Apocalypse, and stating in what respects, and to what extent he had subsequently been led to modify his opinions, and to approximate to Mr. Elliott's.

While thus engaged he was urged to express his opinion of the recent work of Mr. Grattan Guinness,

b

On *The Approaching End of the Age;* and he preferred
to take this opportunity of commenting on it, rather
than attempting formally to review it in a periodical.
Commendation of a work whose merits have so soon
carried it to a fifth Edition would be superfluous, and
to commend an author who has so fully acknowledged
large obligations to himself, might seem out of place.
It has been a great cause of thankfulness to him, to
find his own earlier works on Prophecy utilized and
enforced by so earnest and vigorous a writer, while he
has felt it the more necessary to point out wherein he
differs from his conclusions.

He was anxious also to make his work practically
useful; and with this aim he has added two chapters
on the moral aspects both of belief in the literal fulfilment of prophecy, and of inquiry into the nature of
the times and seasons signified by the prophetic spirit.

Lastly, he found he could no longer be content simply
to restate what his views were when Mr. Elliott miscon-
ceived them, because in one important respect renewed
meditation on the subject had led him to reconsider them,
and thankfully to believe that the predicted limit of
delay of the impending final judgment may be more
distant than he had once supposed. " The Lord is not

slack concerning His promise, but long suffering to us-ward."

He had intended also to make some reply to Canon Farrar's strange and contemptuous denial of the possibility of understanding the apostolic prophecy of the "Man of Sin," but this was rendered unnecessary by a pamphlet recently put forth by the Bishop of Lincoln, which left nothing to be desired.

The sudden stroke of illness which has prevented the author himself from correcting the proofs of the last chapter of the work, has caused the task of supplying the preface to devolve upon his son, who can only commend this little work to the prayerful and reverent consideration of the church, under the blessing of Him from whom cometh all good giving and every perfect gift, with whom is no variableness neither shadow of turning, who is light and in whom is no darkness at all, to whom be the glory for evermore.

Edward B. Birks.

May 20th, 1880.

CONTENTS.

CHAPTER I.

STRUCTURE OF THE APOCALYPSE.

CHAPTER IV.

PROGRESSIVE KNOWLEDGE OF TIMES AND SEASONS.

CHAPTER V.

THE WORLD'S GREAT SABBATH.

THOUGHTS ON THE TIMES AND SEASONS OF SACRED PROPHECY.

CHAPTER I.

STRUCTURE OF THE APOCALYPSE.

FIFTY years have now passed since I began the study of the Prophetic Scriptures. My first printed paper on the subject was in 1833. My first book, " Elements of Prophecy," was published in 1844.

Alike in physical science and in Christian theology, one first requisite for real progress, is to distinguish between first principles, and the superstructure to be raised upon them. Full truth cannot be attained by a sudden bound, but by a gradual progress. In the interpretation of the Apocalypse, the last and crowning message of the Holy Spirit, a law of continuity has been followed in the gradual communication of light and the detection of partial error. Sir Isaac Newton's remark on this subject is quite true: "Among the interpreters of the last age there is scarce one of note who hath not made some discovery worth knowing, whence I gather that God is about opening these mysteries."

My object in the "Elements of Prophecy" was to mark and emphasize the contrast between some first maxims of interpretation, and a superstructure in which there was great diversity of opinion. I showed the great number of consenting authorities, and the direct proof in the testimony of Scripture by which these are confirmed. The book began with the following passage :—

" Ever since the time of the Reformation the following maxims in the interpretation of the sacred prophecies have been generally received by the Protestant Churches.

" 1. That the visions of Daniel commence with the times of the prophet.

" 2. That the events predicted in the Apocalypse begin from the time of the prophecy, or within the first century.

" 3. That the fourth beast (Dan. vii. 7) denotes the Roman Empire.

" 4. That Babylon in the Apocalypse denotes Rome.

" 5. That the little horn in Daniel vii. denotes the Papacy.

" 6. That the ' Man of Sin ' (2 Thess. ii. 3–5 ; Dan. xi. 36–39) relates to the same power.

" 7. That the prophecy in 1 Timothy iv. is fulfilled in past events.

" 8. That Babylon denotes, at least inclusively, Rome papal.

" The three following have also been received by the most learned and able commentators of our own country, from the time of Mede down to the present day :—

" 9. That the two woes (Rev. ix.) relate to the Saracens and the Turks.

" 10. That the two beasts in Revelation xiii. denote the civil and ecclesiastical Latin Empire.

" 11. That a prophetic day denotes a natural year, and a prophetic time three hundred and sixty natural years.

" Of these leading maxims, the four first are held by the Fathers of the Early Church and most of the Roman commentators, as well as by the Reformed Churches. On the other hand, the three last, though generally received by interpreters of the English Church, have been rejected by many foreign Protestants, especially among the Lutheran divines.

"All these maxims, without distinction, have been rejected by the writers commonly called Futurists, and many of them by the writers of the "Tracts for the Times" and their disciples. These writers agree in few points, except in rejecting the conclusions of all previous expositors; and maintain that nearly the whole of Daniel's prophecies and of the Apocalypse are unfulfilled."

These maxims have been received and held in common in the prophetical works of Mr. Cuninghame, Mr. Frere, Mr. Bickersteth, Mr. Faber, Mr. Habershon, Dr. Keith, Dr. Brown, Dr. Fairbairn, Mr. Elliott, Dr. Cumming, Mr. Brookes, and of Mr. Grattan Guinness.

All these maxims, except the 11th, are held also by Bishop Wordsworth in his Commentary on the Apocalypse.

I believe we have now, in 1880, reached the last night watch of the great Saturday of the world's history. The two works of Mr. E. B. Elliott and Mr. Grattan Guinness, the "Horæ Apocalypticæ" (5th edition, 1862), and the "Approaching End of the Age viewed in the Light of Prophecy and Science" (2nd ed., 1879), may be said conjointly to indicate a penultimate stage of prophetical exposition. In the following pages I wish to indicate some of the great truths unfolded in each of these, and some remaining defects, by which a penultimate is naturally differenced from an ultimate and final stage of prophetic interpretation, which can only be reached when the end itself comes.

Mr. Elliott, while he accepts all the maxims given above, has directly reversed one chief aim of my work by the equal and indiscriminate confidence with which he propounds his own conclusions on every secondary topic discussed throughout his four volumes.

My own conviction, after close study of the subject, is, that in his first volume, out of sixty heads he is right in half only; but that in the seventy heads of the three other volumes the error is one-seventh part only; so that about three-fourths of the whole, in my opinion, is sound and true. But the author has fused the whole into one mass, thus lowering the evidence of the firmest and surest parts, where he follows in the wake of a hundred thoughtful and studious writers, to that of novelties in which he claims to have no predecessor, and is likely to have no successor. All uninspired writings however valuable, like earthly food, can only minister to the spiritual life of the Church by a process of digestion, in which some parts are rejected as untrue, or less suited for nourishment, that the rest may become real food, and be transmuted into a part of the human microcosm.

The indiscriminate confidence with which Mr. Elliott propounds all his conclusions alike, on two hundred most difficult and mysterious topics, will repel the great majority of readers, and deter them from paying due attention to his work. Its massive character, amounting virtually to 3600 octavo pages, will concur to the same result. And the smaller class, who can appreciate both the importance of the subject, and the thorough honesty and patient research of the author, are likely to be strongly repelled by its tone of implicit confidence, not only in half a dozen controversies with writers of wholly different views, but in as many more with expositors of past and present generations who agree with him on the main axioms of interpretation, and dissent on secondary questions alone.

I will specify three main questions in which I think Mr. Elliott wholly wrong. The first is the structure of the Apocalypse. The second is his interpretation of the seven Thunders; and the third is his exposition of the first four Trumpets.

I. The Apocalypse consists of seven distinct visions, of which the four last are successive. The three first,— the Seals (ch. iv. 1-viii. 2); the Trumpets (ch. viii. 2-xi. 19); and the vision of the Woman and the Dragon (ch. xii., xiii., xiv.),—are parallel, and range through the whole 2000 years from the time of St. John to the future Judgment. They correspond in the typical history of the fall of Jericho (Josh. vi.),—to the armed host going first; the priests with the trumpets and the ark of the Covenant coming second; and the rereward, including the women and children, following after.

The fourth vision, of the Vials (ch. xv., xvi.), answers to the seven compassings of the seventh day, when the walls of Jericho fell flat. So here at the seventh vial (Rev. xvi. 19) the cities of the nations fall.

The view which Mr. Elliott substitutes is one of three, which have the common feature of confounding together a symbol and the thing symbolized. The first of these views is that of Mr. Cuninghame, who makes the sealed book (Rev. v. 1) identical with the whole Apocalypse. The second is the view of Mede, who makes the little book (Rev. x. 2) to be identical with chapters x., xi. Mr. Elliott makes chapters xii.-xiv. to be identical with the writing on the outside of the sealed book.

But the sealed book and the little book are both of

of them symbols exhibited to the eye of St. John, before the Apocalypse or any part of it was written. To identify either of them with the Apocalypse itself, or with any part of it, involves a confusion very much like that of supposing our own eye to be one part of a landscape it observes.

The second error, that of Mede, almost neutralized the other excellences of his work, and threw back Apocalyptic interpretation for a hundred years after the Reformation. It is one of the excellences of Mr. Elliott's work to have escaped from this error, and to have returned, in his exposition of the tenth and eleventh chapters, to the main current of exposition in the earlier Protestant writers. These with great unanimity apply chapter xi. to the time of the Reformation, and expound the symbol of the little book by the unfolding, and digestion, and open publication, of the Word of God which then took place.

The Sealed Book is plainly a symbol of the whole scheme of Divine Providence, as administered by Christ from the time of the Ascension to the final Judgment. Its being written within and without, and sealed with seven seals, denotes three things. First, its exceeding fulness. Next, that this mighty scheme of redemption and providence could only be realized as the effect and consequence of the adorable sacrifice of the Lamb of God, removing the obstacles which the Divine justice interposed. Thirdly, the writing within and without teaches two things: (1) That it can be only in part known and understood until the whole is accomplished; (2) That even the part fulfilled is too deep and mysterious to be more than partially comprehended by men or angels, or even revealed in Scripture.

Apoc. xii.-xiv. was neither written, nor seen in vision, till the Sealed Book with the writing both within and without, had been seen by the Apostle in the hand of the

Son of Man. The whole vision of the Trumpets also intervenes. The view of Mr. Elliott is thus demonstrably untrue and baseless. I am so far from sharing it, that I have not the least doubt it has rendered his first volume a step backward, and not forward, in the onward march of Apocalyptic interpretation. It wholly distorts the manifold relations of the first half of the prophecy to the Divine type and key in the history of the fall of Jericho.

II. The worst defect however I conceive, in Mr. Elliott's work, is his exposition of the seven Thunders. Though I entirely dissent from Dean Alford's exposition of the Apocalypse, I concur fully in the " surprise and grief" with which he regards this interpretation. I think with him, that "nothing could be more unfortunate" (*Apoc. Alfordiana*, p. 148).

The rash promise of Luther, before the Bull of the Pope appeared condemning his theses, to accept it whenever it should appear as the voice of Christ, he views as a warrant for identifying the seven Thunders, the articulate close of the solemn warning of the glorious angel of the Covenant, with that which, on his own view, is really the voice of the beast from the bottomless pit.

III. The exposition of the first four Trumpets. These really occupy the interval from A.D. 96 to A.D. 622, or from the date of the Apocalypse to that of the Hegira, or the first Woe. Mr. Elliott's false arrangement cuts off the three first centuries from this interval, and delays the commencement of the first Trumpet as late as the reign of Theodosius, A.D. 395. The fourth Trumpet also is wrongly identified with the fall of the Western Empire, A.D. 476. Thus the fulfilment of all the four trumpets, which ranges over five centuries, is crushed within the limit of 80 years only, or one-sixth part of the whole. Thus a series of

uncertain conjectures as to what St. John may have
thought concerning the scenes that may have passed before his eye, wholly takes the place of genuine exposition.

Mr. Elliott's exposition of the last eight chapters
(xv.–xxii.) seems to me a rich repertory of weighty truth,
of vital importance to the Church of Christ in these days,
with only a comparatively small admixture of error. I
regret the errors and defects I have pointed out, chiefly
because I think them very likely to hinder the truths
which form two-thirds of the work, from yielding the full
harvest of blessing and instruction, which they might else
supply to this generation of the Church of Christ.

In this fifth edition I have found, to my great surprise, a whole series of strong affirmations that I have
abandoned and reversed my view of the structure of the
Apocalypse.

His first statement will be found in the very forefront
of the work, in Vol. i., Pref., p. xviii.: "Mr. Birks, the
ablest and most eminent advocate of an historical exposition, founded on a different view of the structure
of the Apocalyptic prophecy from my own, has renounced that counter view; and, both as regards structure, and other points too of minor difference between
us, has acknowledged in fine his substantial agreement
with me." Again, Vol. i. p. 611: "I have mentioned
Mr. Birks's subsequent abandonment of this structural theory, and adoption of the same that I follow myself." Again, Vol. iii. p. 192: "On the points mentioned
in Vol. i. p. 549, Mr. Birks has abandoned his original
view." Vol. iv. p. 557: "Mr. Birks has since then
abandoned the peculiarities of that scheme, and united
himself very much with myself in the general view of
Apocalyptic interpretation."

The view I am said to have abandoned was first developed in a private letter to Archdeacon Hill, and was published at his earnest request in " The Investigator, or Monthly Expositor of Prophecy," in 1833. I there confirmed it by five concurrent arguments. I then expressed my conviction that it was a counterpart in Apocalyptic interpretation to the fundamental doctrine of the Trinity in the Christian system. I said that I felt it a great relief to be landed safely from those tossing waves of doubt as to the structure of the book, which had been so great a snare to the Church.

I now reprint the letter *in extenso*, with the note of Archdeacon Hill. To the views unfolded in it I still adhere.

" ON THE STRUCTURE OF THE APOCALYPSE.

" (*To the Editor of ' The Investigator '*).

" DEAR SIR,—

" The following letter was addressed to me by a friend without the remotest idea of its ever meeting the public eye. Thinking it, however, too valuable a production to be the exclusive property of any individual, I have obtained his permission to offer it for insertion in your excellent Journal.

" That the blessing annexed to the diligent study of the Apocalypse may accompany this effort to ascertain the true principles of interpretation, and to explain the structure of that holy book, is the sincere prayer of your faithful servant,

" T. H.

" DEAR SIR,—

" I feel great pleasure in having any means, however slight, of showing my recollection of your kindness, of which I have had such frequent experience. And as you left with me a sort of request to continue, if I had the opportunity, the subject of my former letter, I do it gladly, feeling that, however imperfect it may be, yet, from the blessing of our common Lord on the study of His Word, and from the increasing interest of these solemn times, you will not feel unacceptable the least hint or aid that may tend to throw light on the Divine Word, and those purposes which are unfolding daily.

"I had begun to speak of the view into which I had been led, of *a twofold fulfilment of Revelation*, which opens so wide and interesting a field to the inquiries of the Church at the present time. I now see that this was hinted at before in Irving's Preface to Ben Ezra, which is indeed full of the seeds of things. The grounds which would lead me to presume this double character are briefly these : First, that we have in 1 Tim. iv. and 2 Tim. iii. two distinct and successive forms of apostasy in the Church, of the 'latter time,' and the 'last days,' in corrupt authorities and selfish lawlessness (marked also in 2 Pet. ii. 10 by the transition "but chiefly"); and which yet are both included by the Apostle under the common title of the 'Man of Sin' to be revealed when the power that let, or the pagan empire, was taken out of the way; and since the Apocalypse is plainly an expansion of the latter prophecy, this of itself is a ground for regarding it as having a twofold character.

"Another, closely connected with this, is the leading object of Revelation, viewed as a history of the appearance, reign, and judgment of Antichrist; just as the gospels contain the birth, the sufferings, and resurrection of Christ. As then the coming of Christ is twofold, viz., in spirit and openly; so is the coming of Antichrist, in spirit first, and then openly. And as in the Old Testament the two advents are frequently linked, not only in succession, (as Isa. xlii., xlix.), but also under common language,—to be first fulfilled in spirit, and then manifestly, (*e.g.* Isa. xl., lxi.),—so is it in harmony with this usage of the Holy Spirit to suppose the same in this great prophecy of the Antichristian power. In this, too, God's providence in His Church is a further confirmation. For as, in these double prophecies mentioned before, the Jewish Church applied them (and with reason) to the coming of Messiah in glory to comfort His people after their long tribulation, and to restore the preserved of Israel; and the Gentile Church applied them, on the warrant of the Spirit, to His coming in humility to comfort the mourners, when a voice from the wilderness prepared His way; so, while the early Church taught, with one voice, the application of the Apocalypse to an infidel Antichrist, whose reign they expected to last for forty-two literal months, the Protestant Church has, with an equally united voice, borne testimony to its application to the mystic or Papal Antichrist in a reign of forty-two mystic months. And if we regard the work itself as of God, and admit the truth of the former application in the Gentile Church at large, I see not how we can refuse its due weight to the latter application, as the witness of the Spirit in the *Protestant* Church. I mention this from having lately met with some clergymen who have begun to give up this latter view entirely, and to discard all past applications of the Apocalypse. This, I am convinced is very erroneous and very injurious; though I nevertheless consider, that there is great strength in their reasons for holding the view of the early Church. The view which I hold seems to me to lighten the whole difficulty; to be in harmony with the whole spirit of revelation, from the first promise in Paradise; and to reconcile most of the many discrepancies, which, without it, would be enough almost to shake the faith of the firmest believer in the blessing, with which our Lord accompanied this holy book when He put it into our hands by His Apostle.

"I had begun, I think, to explain my view of a final application of the seals to the birth and reign of the infidel Antichrist, with the sign announcing his approaching fall. I think I omitted the most striking reference of all, which seems to me to fix it to a future and fast coming accomplishment in the last generation of the Church: I mean, our Lord's noted prophecy, which must find its full and proper accomplishment in that last generation,—the words ἕως ἂν πάντα γένηται (and not πληρωθῇ), denoting an incipient or germinant occurrence, as distinct from a fulfilment. In Luke xxi. 22, 32, the distinction of the words is particularly observable, and seems to be the true key to the meaning, without straining the word "generation" from its natural sense. We have then distinctly *the succession of the Seals in our Lord's prophecy* (Matt. xxiv. 7). For verse 7 answers to the *second, third,* and *fourth* Seals in their order,—war and the sword, famine and pestilence, being marked as the beginning of sorrows, or introductory to the time of great affliction. In verses 9-14, and again 15-24, we have the tribulation itself, answering to the fifth Seal; the time of great tribulation being shortened for the elect's sake (ver. 22), whose cry is heard from beneath the altar in Rev. vi. 10. Then ' *immediately* after the tribulation of those days, the sun shall be darkened, and the moon shall not give her light, and the stars shall fall from the heaven, and the powers of heaven shall be shaken.' The very signs, and almost the very words, of the *sixth* Seal (Rev. vi. 12–14), after which ensues the coming of Christ and the wrath of the Lamb.

" Before proceeding further, however, I feel it necessary to turn to a subject which naturally precedes the above; viz., the *structure* of the Apocalypse. For if the visions of this Divine book have to bear the weight of a double interpretation, it becomes the more necessary to assure ourselves of their arrangement and mutual relation; else, in proportion to the fulness we assign them, will be the danger of confusion. I had, as you are aware, studied and received the views of Mr. Frere on the structure of the Apocalypse. Of their general truth I felt strongly persuaded; but I determined to sift them afresh in every part, resting on the one principle of seeking in Scripture itself the key to its own meaning, and receiving no principle as certain till I could see a distinct reason and warrant for it in the word of God. The consequence has been, in the main, a far stronger conviction and certainty than I could have entertained before, when several things were taken, as it were, on trust; but on one point an important modification.

" I will just briefly state the views of former writers, and then my own; which I will then confirm by reasons both within the Apocalypse and from the rest of Scripture, which have grown upon me as I have reflected, and several of which I have not seen alluded to before.

" Mede, then, regards the Seals and Trumpets as one consecutive series down to chapter x., where he makes a new prophecy begin with the 'little book,' which first

runs through the whole course of time in the eleventh;
and again in the three following chapters. The vials he
places under the sixth Trumpet, except the last vial, which
he makes to coincide with the seventh Trumpet.

".Bp. Newton divides the whole into two series, one
from chapters iv. to xi., and then from chapter xii. onward. Cuninghame, setting out with the axiom that the
seven-sealed Book is the Apocalypse, and therefore that
the Seals contain the whole, interprets the first six as
carrying us down to the time of the Advent, and the
seventh as revealing and including the rest; viz., the
Trumpets to the tenth chapter, the 'little book' in the
eleventh, the Church history in chapters xii.-xiv.; and the
Vials, which he views as poured out all at once, under the
seventh Trumpet and sixth Seal, the earthquake of which
he regards as the same with that of the seventh Vial.

"I may observe, in passing, that two of the three
series,—the Seals and the Vials,—are thus broken up
from their natural order, and each in a different manner.
Mr. Frere views the prophecy as three parallel streams;
(1) the Seals, chapters v.-vii.; (2) the Trumpets, chapters
viii.-x.; (3) the 'little book' itself twofold, first in chapter xi., with the seventh Trumpet introduced for the sake
of synchronism, and secondly in chapters xii. to xiv.,
followed by the Vials, and then by three explanatory
visions, chapters xvii. 1; xix. 10; xxi. 9; xxii. 15. In
this last I concur, with one important change, the
principle of which I will explain.

"Mr. Cuninghame and Mr. Frere seem to me both to
have erred, in common with most commentators since
Mede, in making the sealed and open books to be *the
Apocalypse,* or parts of the Apocalypse, instead of being,
like all the rest, *emblems* set before the Prophet, in those

visions of the Apocalypse which he records, and the meaning of which is to be sought *objectively*, as objects in the
vision, not *subjectively*, as parts of the prophecy, which
is plainly written by the Prophet in succession, while
the visions proceed (Rev. x. 4).

"The confusion resulting from this, is like that of
conceiving your own eye to be one of the objects in the
landscape; and has arisen from the verbal spirit which
has overrun the Protestant Church, from studying the
Bible as a *book*, instead of viewing it as a *record*, and
transporting ourselves in spirit into the scenes it sets
before us. The meaning of those emblems I think very
striking and beautiful, but cannot at present stop to
explain.

"I will now mention that arrangement of the Revelation
which I think demonstrably true, both from internal and
external evidence, and which its very simplicity recommends. We have, then, three parallel streams of vision:
the *Seals*, in chapters v., vi., and vii., with viii. 1; the
Trumpets, in chapters viii., ix., x., and xi., including the
first part of what Frere, Mede, and others call the
Biblaridion; and the *Church history*, chapters xii. to xiv.;
followed by the Vials, chapters xv., xvi., and then by
three answering visions or explanations, as before. Thus,
at once, the Trumpets are left unbroken in order; and the
threefold principle of arrangement (or sevenfold for the
whole Apocalypse) is restored; which, by Mr. Frere, is
partly broken by his *double* series of the 'little book.'
By this change, too, the connection of chapters x., xi.,
and the change of tense and person in the latter (see
verses 1, 3, 4, 10, 11,—confessedly the most obscure part
of the Apocalypse, and usually passed over with little
remark), has opened upon me in its clearness and

beauty; and I may further remark (though anticipating
the subject of particular interpretation), that one great
stumbling-block in Mr. Frere's system, viz., its including no mention of the. Reformation, as such, is thereby
removed.

" I will first examine separately two important points of
the prophecy, where the above view diverges from Mede,
Cuninghame, and Faber,—and in the latter point from
Mr. Frere also, and from most other recent commentators,
—and then proceed with direct proofs of its general pro-
priety and truth. These two are the separation and commencement afresh at chapter viii. 1, and the continuity of
the prophecy in chapters x., xi. In the combination of
these two the peculiarity mainly resides, for it differs
from most modern writers except Vitringa and Frere in
the first, and from the latter in the second. In both
these, the error I conceive has arisen from the cause
mentioned above—the study of the Apocalypse as a book,
and not as a record.

" Now, in chapter viii. 1, if we read it merely as a book,
nothing can be closer than its connection with what
follows, or more entire than its separation from what precedes. I observe then, first, that as the whole time of
the visions seen by the Apostle was clearly the space of a
single day, prophetic intervals of time are never repre-
sented as passing in the vision, but are simply stated for
the information of the Church, when, for the very purpose
of avoiding incongruity, there is a change from vision
to narrative, and then to vision again. The silence,
therefore, of chapter viii. 1, is unique, being unlike all
other times mentioned, which are prophetic statements
for our information. This is an absolute pause in the
course of the visions; a pause as of half an hour in visions

that lasted at the most through a single day, perhaps only part of a day. If, then, instead of reading the *book*, we enter into the spirit of the *record*, the mark of a close and recommencement of the visions would be as striking as if our eye, in reading, met with a blank of half a page. The positive signs of such a transition will come afterwards; but the above remark, I think, wholly turns the weight of presumption in favour of the separation, since we can conceive no other reason for which such a pause should be made. A rest in the prophetic actions being never so denoted, but by some voice (as chapter xi. 12) expressing an interval of time.

"I pass on to the second keystone in the above arrangement, viz., the *continuity* of the prophecy in chapters x. and xi.; and seeing the proofs of this so numerous and clear as I now do, and the application so simple and unembarrassed; I wonder the more, both at myself for not having perceived this sooner, and at the number of commentators who follow each other in the forced separation. I have scarcely read enough to know the exceptions; but most, I think, of our Protestant commentators since Mede have followed him in this, making the 'little book' a separate and integral part of the prophecy, which some close with chapter xi., others with chapter xiv. The same principle as before is involved in this error. For if we once consider the vision itself, we find ourselves inextricably entangled by such a view. The Prophet had seen the seven angels standing prepared to sound,—had heard six of their trumpets blown,—had seen the sixth angel in vision loose the angels in the Euphrates, the seventh still standing with his trumpet not yet sounded;—had heard this mighty angel declare with an oath, that in the days of his trumpet the mystery of God

c

should be finished. He is now called on himself to take a part in the vision, and from a silent recorder to become an actor in the great scene;—after which he sees the great earthquake and the fall of one tenth of the city;—and now the second woe is past, and the third woe cometh quickly. The seventh angel, who till now had stood prepared to sound (ch. viii. 6), but had not yet sounded, gives the final blast, and the voice of triumph is heard in heaven. Once let us realize the seven angels with their trumpets standing in the Prophet's view, and we can scarce avoid the conviction that the course of the vision is unbroken.

" And if we examine thoroughly the reasons which have led so many to an opposite judgment, they will each confirm this view instead of disproving it. The first is the synchronism of the voice of the mighty angel with the sounding of the seventh trumpet, and of the seven thunders with the vials; and the action of taking possession of the earth and sea answering to the ascription,— ' Thou hast taken to Thee Thy great power, and hast reigned.' All this agreement I deem most true and close; with this further remark, that it is the agreement not of a symbolic fact, but of a prophetic warning, with its fulfilment. And this is marked doubly; first, by the voice from heaven, instructing the Prophet to seal the seven thunders and not write them : and secondly, by the oath of the angel, which plainly speaks of the voice of the seventh angel, and the close of the mystery of God as still future, while announcing them to be near.

"It has caused much perplexity why the thunders should be mentioned, if their voices were not to be known. But the true key lies, I doubt not, in a circumstance frequently overlooked; viz., that the sealing of a prophecy in Scripture denotes properly, not its *concealment* from the knowledge of the Church, but a season of *delay* in its fulfilment in the sight of the world. Compare the reasons assigned Dan. viii. 26; xii. 4, 9, 10; Rev. xxii. 10, with Isaiah viii. 16, and I think this will plainly appear, though I have not time to dwell upon it. By means of this view, however, the passage before us becomes perfectly simple; and we see its meaning to be, that though the voice of these thunders was near at hand, there would be first a pause of delay, till another warning should be given, and since the voice of the angels of providence had been in vain, a mightier voice should be given by the ministry of the word.

" The next circumstance which has led to the belief of a separation, is the words of the angel to the Prophet, supposed to imply a re-commencement of the vision. But we must observe, that though the Prophet had been recording the visions, he could in no proper sense be said to have been prophesying, while a silent spectator of the great and awful scene. The whole spirit of the passage, as it seems to me, is thus lost, and its application, which otherwise flashes on the mind at once, is totally obscured. Let us trace the words closely.

" The Prophet is commanded to prophesy again, which implies a *former* prophesying. Till now he had been only a silent spectator, with awe-struck spirit recording the visions; and the mystery of the voice is, that now the Prophet is to be no longer a mere spectator, but himself to take a part in the scene, and become one of the very emblems which he himself records. And what then is the former prophesying alluded to? For this we must ascend beyond the visions, during which his voice has been hushed and still: and we find Rev. i. 9, that at this very time, while favoured with these very visions, the aged seer was a lonely exile, 'in the isle that is called Patmos, for the word of God, and for the testimony of Jesus Christ.' But though he was thus already suffering for the truth's sake ; yet when, after the fearful warnings of the two former woes, the demon worshippers still refuse to repent, the perilous and hard commission is given to this last of the apostles,—' to prophesy again, before many peoples and nations and tongues and kings.' The work was dangerous, but the necessity was great. The warnings of the angels and the voice of providence had passed unheeded. The rest of the men still repented not of their deeds ; the wrath of Judah's Lion is aroused; and thus the emphasis of the charge, 'thou *must needs* (δεῖ σε πάλιν,) prophesy again, etc.' To confirm this view still more strikingly, compare Amos iii. 5–8, to which it seems directly to refer us : ' *The lion hath roared*, who will not fear? The Lord God hath spoken, *who can but prophesy ?* '

" The subject is so wide I must pass hastily over the other head, viz., the period of 1260 days, which has been viewed as another reason for regarding the prophecy as recommenced. I observe only, that by the change of tense in the word ἐδόθη, it is implied that the treading down had already begun, which must continue till its *whole* time be accomplished ; and so with the coeval prophesying of the Witnesses, though the *giving of power* was then to begin.

"One more remark I may make to close the whole proof of continuity. Though before the descent of the mighty angel, ' the remnant of the men repented not ; ' yet before the second woe passes away, ' the remnant

were affrighted, and gave glory to the God of heaven ; '
upon which, and not till then, it is said, ' the third woe
cometh quickly.'

" I fear I shall have wearied your patience, though I
I strive to compress ; but the arrangement of the Apocalypse lies so much at the root of all quiet conviction on
the subject of its meaning, the variety of comments and
of views of its structure and application, has been so great
a handle both to open enemies and to careless professors,
and faith in the promised blessing has with many waxed
so faint and dim, that I feel it myself to be a great relief
to be landed safely from those tossing waves of doubt as
to its connection and meaning, and spiritual benefit, which
have been so great a snare to the Church, and so great
an engine of Satan.   And feeling this, you will bear with
me, if I appear somewhat prolix on points which might
else seem technical and subordinate, but which once
settled, the structure of the whole comes out with ease
and clearness.

" But though the determination of these two points,
on account of their distinctive character, seemed desir-
able, yet the direct proofs, both within the Apocalypse
and in the rest of Scripture, confirming that view of
arrangement which results from adopting them, and its
important bearing on the great heads of Christian doctrine, and especially the threefold dominion of the Three
Persons of the Godhead administered by the Son of Man,
are not few.   But into this wide and interesting field
I cannot enter, but throw out the hint, in passing, for
your maturer consideration.   My space and time compel
me to limit myself to the internal proofs afforded by
the Apocalypse itself.   These will result from comparing
the three visions in their beginning, their continuance,

and their close; the place of the fourth, as succeeding them, then results immediately.

"First then, in their *beginning* ; the three visions each open with the introduction of fresh symbolical agents, not seen by the Apostle before. Thus, in the general preface of chapter xiv., though the living creatures and elders are seen, the more dignified person, ' the Lamb of God,' is not witnessed till the vision of the seals is introduced by the book seen in the hand of Him 'who sitteth upon the throne;' and the Lamb is then first seen in the vision, appearing to receive and open it. In like manner the second vision opens with the words, ' And I saw the seven angels which stand before God.' These also, the agents in the trumpet vision, as the Lamb Himself in the vision of the seals, the Prophet had not witnessed till then ; the seven lamps of fire (ch. iv. 5), being in all likelihood distinct in meaning, and evidently a different emblem. And thus also the third vision opens with words implying a recommencement; and the Prophet has a fresh person in vision brought before his view : ' a woman clothed with the sun,' the leading sufferer in this vision of patient suffering : as the Lamb and the seven angels were the leading agents in the former visions of active judgment. This is the first simple and very distinct proof that these are three parallel visions.

"The next is closely connected. Not only does each vision open with some great symbolical person or persons, but in its opening it presents our Lord Himself under distinct emblems. Thus in the *first* He appears as the Lamb with seven horns and seven eyes ; in the *second* as the Angel of the Covenant, offering the prayers of the saints with much incense on the altar of God ; and in the *third* as the Man-Child, caught up to God and His throne, who is to rule all the nations with a rod of iron. This is a second proof and resembles the former.

"The *third* proof is, that each vision near its commencement adopts and embodies one of three similar prophecies of our Lord (Mat. x. 34). 'Think not that I am come to send peace on the earth : I came not to send peace but a sword ; ' accordingly in the second seal, ' there went out another horse that was red, and power was given to him that sat thereon to take *peace* from the earth, and that they should kill one another; and *there was given unto him a great sword.*' The next is Luke xii. 49, closely connected with the former. 'I am come to *cast fire upon the earth,* and what will I if it be already kindled ! ' And thus, ere the 'seven angels prepared themselves to sound,' the angel ' took *fire* from the altar, and cast it upon the earth, and there were voices and thunderings and lightnings and an earthquake ! ' Finally, in Luke x. 18, our Lord declares in prophecy : ' I beheld Satan as lightning fall from heaven.' And in the vision of the sun-clothed woman, ' the great dragon was cast out into the earth, and his angels were cast out with him,' and the loud voice of victory is heard in heaven. This triple mark then of correspondence meets us in the opening of the visions.

"There is a further mark of unity running throughout each vision, which you would perhaps become sensible of by reading each with a pause between. In the first then (Rev. v. 1), our Lord having been introduced under the symbol of the Lamb, He neither appears nor is mentioned under any other. In the vision of the *trumpets* (viii. 2), on the contrary, He is never either introduced or mentioned under that emblem, but only as the Christ in His threefold office of *Priest*, of *Prophet* (which again confirms the former view of those verses), and of *Lord* and *King*. Again in the vision of the bride (ch. xii. 1), which coexists with the other two, and yet has a peculiar character of its own,—our Lord is introduced under both the former emblems ; and also under a third, peculiar to this vision, viz., as the 'Son of Man,' born to rule all nations with a rod of iron; and again appears in the same character at its close, as if to clasp together its various parts into one united whole.

" Perhaps it may serve also further to mark the unity and harmony of each vision, by a common sevenfold character, that as the former are distinctly divided by seven seals, and seven trumpets, so even in this last, which is a vision of continuous and unbroken suffering, the number of heavenly messengers is also seven, three angels of warning, the Son of Man, and three angels from the temple and the altar (ch. xiv.) at the close.

"And now it only remains to add the marks of synchronism between the close of these and the opening of the vials. These are mainly two; the signs of the day of wrath and the trump of jubilee ; the ingathering of the harvest and the feast of tabernacles. It will thus also appear, on comparing the order of the Levitical feasts, that the seventh trumpet precedes by a short space the seventh seal; the former being, in its final acceptation, the signal of the resurrection of the saints ; and the latter following their voices of triumph, and opening the series of those last plagues, in which they have power given them over the nations to execute upon them the judgment written—'This honour have all His saints.'

" Thus, my dear sir, have I laid before you those views

of the structure of this divine and mysterious book, to which after much meditation I have been led, and which I regard as the basis of a just interpretation; both in its application to the past history of Providence, which I conceive to be now near its close under the seventh vial; and in its application to fast approaching warnings and judgments; when, after the overthrow of. the papal Babylon, like paganism of old, we are to be led, as I judge, through sword and famine and pestilence to that short hour of great tribulation, from which the Son of Man Himself shall deliver us. Oh how hard it is to hold fast this faith, when the temptations to the false peace of the world are so strong on every side! But, blessed be His name! ' Whatsoever is born of God overcometh the world; and this is the victory, even our faith.'

" I fear I shall not find time at present to pursue this deeply interesting subject, either in the confirmation, which I think may be found from five or six different sources in the Old Testament, of the leading principles above; or in the past or mystic application of the prophecy; or in its future and more open form. The confidence I have in the truth of the latter, is confirmed by the return which seems to be beginning towards the early doctrine of the Church on this head; but it chiefly rests on the unimpeached and full testimony it receives in all its parts, or almost all, from the Old Testament prophecies, or from that of our Lord. I may just mention, as a kind of confirmation of 'this, and very satisfactory to my own mind, that though differing from Mr. Cuninghame so much in point of principles of arrangement, yet nearly all of his latest conclusions on the future aspect and series of changes connected with the blessed advent of our Lord (laid down by him in the preface to one of his pamphlets, and which he extracts with some difficulty by a minute collation of separate passages), I had been led to before, with great simplicity and more detail from the view alluded to above."

  * * * * * *

The same view as in the above letter of 1833, was emphatically reaffirmed in my work the "MYSTERY OF PROVIDENCE" (published in 1848), in express contrast to Mr. Elliott's own view. I said that the vision, chap. vii., " resists decisively every effort to apply it to the times of Constantine, and still more to those of Augustine ; and referring us plainly to the type in the Feast of Tabernacles, fixes its own application to the ingathering of the whole Church after the great tribulation of the last days."

I quote the following passage from the Preface. "The present volume contains an exposition of the 8th and 9th chapters of the Apocalypse, which form the main part of the Trumpet vision. Some apology for its publication is perhaps necessary, when so many works on that Divine prophecy, by eminent writers, have appeared within the last few years. Besides the ' Sacred Calendar ' of Mr. Faber, the Expositions of Mr. Cuninghame and Mr. Habershon, and the ' Signs of the Times ' by Dr. Keith, with expositions of an entirely different class by Dr. Todd, Professor Stuart, and others ; the ' Horæ Apocalypticæ ' has gained of late a high and deserved reputation. No previous commentary has brought such various materials to bear on the historical explanation of the visions ; and none, perhaps, has left the impression of its substantial truth, or even of its minute accuracy, on a wider circle of readers. . . .

Hence not a few may be ready to apply to Mr. Elliott's learned and valuable work the legendary saying of the caliph respecting the Koran, and to decide that any other exposition, if it agrees with it, is superfluous, and presumptuous wherever it differs. Those, also, who are aware of the sceptical feeling, among too many Christians, relative to this holy prophecy, created by the number and diversity of past expositions, may fear that every fresh work will only aggravate the evil; that its partial divergence from previous writers will more than neutralize its substantial agreement, and confirm the prejudices of those who despise all such interpretations as the dreams of fancy.

"These reasons have some weight, but appear to me greatly outweighed by others of an opposite kind. The first of these relates to points of agreement with previous expositions. It is a maxim of the Divine law, that 'in the mouth of two or three witnesses shall every word be established.' The publication of any exposition, of which the main principle is radically false, can hardly fail to be injurious; and even the multiplication of mere copies, where the views of another are received almost with implicit faith, tends much more to the diffusion than the confirmation of the original system. But the case is very different with mature convictions, independently formed, by those who have bestowed on the subject a close and careful study. In our present dimness of faith and spiritual discernment, it cannot be expected that even such students should entirely agree in their views upon every part of so mysterious a prophecy. It is only when that which is perfect is come, that partial insight will be replaced by a full and complete unity of judgment in these deep things of God.

But until we attain that happy and holy state, there is
nothing which tends more powerfully to confirm the faith
of Christians in this prophecy, and at the same time
to awaken a spirit of inquiry, than substantial agreement,
in the main features of its interpretation, among those
who show clearly, by their partial divergence, that they
have thought carefully for themselves, and not followed
blindly in the track of others.   It is such an agreement
of witnesses, in courts of law, which constitutes the most
convincing testimony; and a similar consent of expositors amidst minor diversities must have a like effect, with
honest and serious minds, in this difficult field of prophetic interpretation.   Those who only desire excuses for
unbelief or contempt of God's word, will never fail to
discover them ; but the effect, on all those who look below
the surface, will be to confirm, and not to weaken their
faith, in the Divine inspiration and historical fulfilment
of this holy prophecy.

"Next, with regard to those minor diversities themselves, it is clear that if truth is to be attained and
widely received in the details of exposition, this must be
accomplished, not by concealing differences of judgment
with a studied silence, so as to create an appearance of
greater unity than really exists, but by a free, sober, and
reverent discussion.   Such a course, if only pursued with
Christian humility, in the spirit of brethren who delight
to agree and are sorry to differ, can hardly fail to aid
the establishment of truth, while its development will be
richer and more varied from the cross-lights obtained by
the thoughts of many minds.   This is the Divine law,
in prophetic truth, as in natural science.   One may be
privileged with a larger share than others, but no one
has a monopoly in these treasures of Divine wisdom.

'Many shall run to and fro, and knowledge shall be increased.'

"The present volume has been written, and is now offered to the public, as a contribution, however unworthy, to this great and noble object. The outline of the whole was written before those other works of the author on prophecy, which have been already published, and have met with a very encouraging acceptance from the Christian public. Aware, however, that Mr. Faber's 'Sacred Calendar of Prophecy' was just being republished, and that the 'Horæ Apocalypticæ' was about soon to appear, the author purposely turned aside to other parts of the same general field of prophecy, where it seemed that his labour would be more usefully bestowed. After the appearance of that learned and valuable work, which few can esteem more highly, the whole has not only been re-written, but subjected to a second revision, that it might present only the results of patient and deliberate judgment. Having done this, the opinion of valued friends as well as his own impression, led him to hope that the time was come when its publication would not be rash or premature, and might, with the blessing of God, be useful to the Church of Christ in these eventful times.

"The distinctive features of the work, which chiefly encourage him to indulge this hope are the following. First, instead of embracing the whole prophecy, a portion is selected, where the substantial agreement of Protestant interpreters is, perhaps, the greatest; and where the character of the emblems implies a peculiar publicity and prominence in the events to which they relate. The series in respect of time, within the limit thus chosen, is unbroken and continuous, and is therefore favourable to unity of impression from the whole work. Next, the same circumstance has allowed a greater fulness in the direct historical interpretation; so that the vision is brought into close comparison, not with a few general facts, but with the whole course of Roman history. In the third place, the interpretation, I believe, has this distinguishing feature, that the emblems of the vision, explained in the most natural sense, and compared with the whole body of national history, as presented by the best and ablest historian of the Roman empire, will be found throughout in exact and unbroken accordance. Other expositors have frequently selected a few passages from Gibbon, where his expressions illustrate their views of the prophecy. But the correspondence which it has been endeavoured to establish in the present work, is far more extensive and complete. A proof is thus exhibited that the word of God is the key of all providence; and that these chapters contain in miniature, like a landscape painted on the retina, the whole course of the Decline and Fall of the Roman Empire.

" The chief point where the view here adopted diverges from the ' Horæ,' is in the relation of the Seals and Trumpets."

In the Introduction to the same work the following passage occurs.

" The prophecy, as here explained, is composed of seven distinct, but closely related visions, of which the three first are mainly parallel with each other. These three streams of prediction are reunited in the fourth vision, of the Seven Vials, and are then continued in three distinct, successive parts, in the closing chapters of the book. On the view here preferred, and which has been the more usual and prevalent ever since the first centuries, the

Seals and Trumpets are two closely connected series of prophetic history, parallel in the times to which they relate, with distinct and appropriate symbols in each series, that retain throughout their own proper meaning. The former will refer to the great, silent, organic changes of Divine Providence, and the latter to wars, tumults, and convulsions, and the whole course of audible and conspicuous judgments. The vision which succeeds to them, in like manner, will relate to the trials and deliverances of the spiritual Church; while they all converge on one great crisis ; the final overthrow of the powers of evil, the bridal of the Church, and the manifested kingdom of our Lord Jesus Christ.

" The vision of the Seals is thus an outline of the work of redemption, in its silent and irreversible progress, often hidden in gloom and darkness, till it issues in the full triumph of Divine grace, and the gathering of an innumerable company of ransomed ones, in the great Feast of Tabernacles, around the throne."

I have further argued out the truth of the same view in pp. 50–60 of the same work, and pp. 100–106.

My full persuasion of its truth was the ground on which I based the whole work, a volume of 450 pages.

The same view, expressly derived from me, is given in Mr. Bickersteth's " Practical Guide to the Prophecies " (6th edition, 1844), in contrast to Mr. Elliott's view, and continued to its 8th edition, 1852, the year after the publication of Mr. Elliott's 4th edition.

It there enters doubly in ten pages of direct argument, pp. 231–240, followed by four pages of more detailed statement. I reproduce it here, the work being, like those above cited, out of print.

" The author," says Mr. Bickersteth, " after considering the vast variety of interpretations which have been given of this difficult, but truly precious book, most acquiesces in views in which he has been assisted by his valued friend, Mr. Birks, which he gives briefly in this chapter. . . .

"First, the systems of Faber, Cuninghame, and Frere agree alike with Mede and Bengel, in the following principles. The commencement of the prophecy in the time of St. John. Its continuance to the end of all things, without intervening break or chasm; the future and literal millennium; the application of the first four trumpets to judgments in the third, fourth, and fifth centuries; the prediction of the Saracens in one of the two former woes; the future restoration of Israel; the application of the woman to the true Christian Church; an express description of the Papacy, in chapter xiii.; the mystical reckoning of the times, chapters xii., xiii.; the short and rapid succession of the vials; the application of Babylon to the Roman church; its future destruction by ten kings; the rebuilding of Jerusalem, the holy city, and the Temple of God. . . .

"Secondly. Faber, Cuninghame and Frere agree with Mede, where he differs from Bengel, in the following points. The agreement in time, of the seventh trumpet with the vials; the application of the first woe to the Saracens; the application of the second woe to the Turks; the application of the first beast to the secular Latin empire; the application of the second beast to the ecclesiastical Latin empire; the common mystical reckoning of the forty-two months and 1260 days, chapters xi., xii., xiii.; the place of chapter xi. before the seventh trumpet; the rate of the mystical reckoning, a year for a day; the mystical meaning of the holy city, chapter

xi. 2; the death and resurrection of the witnesses; the priority of the earthquake (xi. 13) to the seventh trumpet, and to the earthquake (xvi. 16). . . .

"Since these remarks were written, my friends Mr. Habershon's and Mr. Elliott's valuable contributions to the elucidation of this sacred book have appeared. Mr. Habershon's is calculated for general and popular usefulness, and Mr. Elliott's for critical and fuller investigation.

"I need not say that I prize both. Mr. Elliott's work is especially important, and though differing in our views of the structure of this book and some of the details; we agree substantially in the general interpretation, and especially as to the position in which we now stand. But I must here notice rather those parts of the interpretation in which we have differed, and I regret to add, still differ. . . .

"With his view of the arrangement, or structure of the Apocalypse, I am unable to concur. I cannot see that the sealed book was fulfilled before the time of Constantine, or that it comprehends more of the prophecy than chapters v., vi., vii. This part of the prophecy is continued, as it appears to me, in chapters xix. and xx., where we have many parallels to show connection and continuance. . . . I view the seals as describing the whole Christian dispensation till our Lord's return; and I consider that we are now in the pause of judgment connected with the Sixth Seal, from the withholding of the winds, Rev. vii. It appears to me that we have seen the events pointed out at the beginning of the Sixth Seal, where is set before us a figurative description of the French Revolution. When the withholding of the winds ceases, it will probably pass to the literal description of visible events connected with the

D

return of our Lord from heaven, as so often brought before us in reference to that event. Matt. xxiv. 29; Luke xxi. 25.

" It may be useful, however, to dwell more fully on the most important part of the subject, where the interpretation of Mr. Elliott diverges from those which have been stated above. In the application of the Seals, he forsakes the arrangement of Woodhouse, Cuninghame, Vitringa and most of the early writers, and reverts to the hypothesis of Mede, in an approved and modified form. They are thus applied to political changes from Trajan to Constantine, and not to the history of the visible church through the whole dispensation. A separate appendix is devoted to a refutation of the other view.

" It would be too long a task to enter fully into this question. It will be enough to state briefly the main reasons which appear decisive against this contracted range of the seals, and to remove one or two objections against the rival interpretation.

" 1. First, the great tribulation (chap. vii. 14), is a clear proof that the seals reach to the time of the end. For both in Matt. xxiv. and Dan. xii. 1, this tribulation is placed immediately before the Advent, and the resurrection of those who are sleeping in the dust. The words are emphatic,—the tribulation, the great one,— clearly alluding to the declaration of our Lord, first in vision to Daniel, and then to His disciples on earth. There is no mark whatever of anticipation in the vision, but the reverse. It is when the sealing angel has returned and given his report of the numbers, that this ingathering succeeds; which is a clear token that the end of the dispensation is then come.

" 2. A second proof may be found in the palm-bearing

multitude. For the description is plainly the antitype of the last day in the feast of tabernacles under the law. This is commonly allowed, and becomes plain on comparing the texts. Now this feast was 'in the end of the year, when they had gathered in the fruits of the earth.' It followed close on the harvest. And hence the event in chap. vii. must follow the harvest described in Rev. xiv. 14–16. The great day of the feast also followed the jubilee trumpet in the Day of Atonement. And hence the same ingathering (Rev. vii.) must refer to the time of the seventh Trumpet, the season of jubilee and deliverance to the Church of God.

"3. The type in Ezek. ix., x., confirms the same view. The sealing there lasts while the six angels of slaughter execute judgment. The number sealed is then reported, and the last stroke of judgment follows. Now the six messengers of slaughter clearly answer to the angels of the six first trumpets in Revelation. But the ingathering (ch. vii.) follows the report of the number sealed, and therefore is after six trumpets have sounded, and when the seventh is close at hand.

"4. The symmetry of the whole series demands the same view. For as Vitringa remarks, 'reason seems to require that this sealed volume, distinguished into seven books, should exhibit the events in such order as to bear the traces of a divine proportion in the distribution of times. But no such order or proportion is found in an interpretation, which makes the emblems of the six former seals bring us only to the times of Constantine, and the seventh include the events of all after ages, the end of which is still to come.'

"5. The nature of the prophetic emblems leads to the same conclusion. For the angel with the censer plainly .

denotes our Lord Himself. But it is quite incongruous that our Lord should be presented in the vision at the same time as the Lamb holding the sealed book, and as an angel in the Lamb's presence at the altar. Hence in viii. 2, the emblem of the Lamb must have disappeared, which is confirmed by the whole series of the Trumpets. A distinct vision has thus begun, and the series of the seals is completed before the angel appears at the altar.

" 6. The fundamental type of the fall of Jericho, confirms all these indications. There were three parts of the army of Israel—the armed men going first, the seven priests with seven trumpets before the ark, and the rereward of women and children following after. The second of these plainly typifies the seven trumpets with the ark of the covenant revealed at their close (xi. 19). The third equally answers to the vision of the Woman, the Man-child, and the remnant of her seed. Therefore the armed men going before have their counterpart in the vision of the Seals and the celestial Horsemen. And hence we may derive two conclusions. First, the seals, like the two series that followed, extend throughout the dispensation. And next, the event which completes their series is the appearing of the armies in heaven (ch. xix.) for the final victory.

" 7. The natural meaning of the emblem points to the same view. For if the book sealed with seven seals imports that Divine Providence is shrouded in deep mystery, the opening of the last seal must equally import that the mystery is ended, and a time of manifestation is begun. Hence it must be parallel with the time of the seventh angel, in whose days ' the mystery of God shall be finished.' And this explains why the events of the seventh seal should not be recorded under its opening. For then the character of mystery ceases. The events which then follow belong to the manifestation of Christ's kingdom, and hence are more naturally referred to the trumpet vision, where the character of the emblems imports open and visible acts of judgment and deliverance.

" This remark serves to meet the only objection of real weight, the apparently maimed character of the seventh seal, when the trumpets are made to commence a new series. Here we need only to distinguish between the times themselves which are symbolized and the symbolic record. The times of the seventh seal are those also of the seventh trumpet, and are given with the fullest detail in chapters xix. and xx. But the symbolic record is suspended for this very reason, that the Seals are an emblem importing mystery and its removal : and at the seventh seal the mystery ceases, and the events need to be pourtrayed under a different emblem, the blast of a trumpet-angel, or the opening, not of a seal, but of heaven itself.

" On this view also, the moral harmony is complete. The series of the four horsemen, as denoting the visible Church in successive stages, after being obscured for a time by its foul degeneracy, breaks forth anew in more than its original glory, when the armies in heaven are seen following the Word of God, clothed in fine linen, clean and white. The horsemen themselves, the cry of the martyrs, the white robes given to them, the alarm and consternation of the kings of the earth (vi. 11), are thus, all crowned and completed in the events of the latter vision (ch. xix.), which really belongs to the time of the seventh seal ; for then only the mystery of God is finished, and the manifestation of the Divine glory

is begun. Let the reader compare diligently the har-
monies of chapters iv., v., vi. and vii., with chapters xix.
and xx. and he will see how fully chapters xix. and xx.
correspond to the sealed book, and complete its visions
in the promised glory of the Church of Christ.

" The continuance of the times of the seven seals in the
19th chapter, and the parallelisms of that chapter with
them may be seen by this comparison. The silence described (viii. 1) is broken, xix. 1. The emblem of the
white horse (vi. 2) appears again, xix. 11. The testimony
given (vi. 9) appears also, xiv. 10. The kings, captains,
etc., all in terror (vi. 16), are vanquished, xix. 16.
The judgment delayed (vi. 10), is executed, xix. 2. The
robes made white in the blood of the Lamb (vii. 9) are
mentioned again, xix. 8, 14. The horses describing the
Church militant (xi. 2, 4, 5, 8) appear again, but all
white, with the elders clothed in fine linen, xix.

" Unquestionably the sealed book is, as might be expected from its deeply mysterious character, and from
the plain statement, that "no man in heaven, nor in
earth, nor under the earth, was able to open the book,
neither to look thereon," the most difficult part of the
whole prophecy. But as the attention of the Church of
Christ is more prayerfully and closely directed to it, it will
assuredly be more and more opened, to the full satisfaction
of all who seek the blessing promised to those who
study this blessed book."

GENERAL AXIOMS OF INTERPRETATION OF THE APOCALYPSE.

I.—*General Scope.*

" 1. The Apocalypse is a prophecy of things which
were still future in the time of the Apostle.

2. It is a prophecy reaching to the end of all things, and the eternal kingdom of Christ.

3. The opening vision, in the address to the Seven Churches, relates to things which were then present. Ch. i. 19.

4. The angelic vision, ch. iv. 1–xii., relates to things which were next to follow.

5. The prophecy is continuous between these two limits.

6. The four beasts, Dan. vii., denote the Babylonian, Medo-Persian, Grecian, and Latin or Roman Empires.

7. The coming of the Son of Man, Dan. vii., is the second advent of Christ.

8. The kingdom of the Son of Man, Dan. vii., is a future visible, earthly and glorious kingdom of Christ.

9. The Judgment, Rev. xix., is the same with that in Dan. vii.

10. The vision, Rev. xix., refers to the second coming of Christ.

11. The millennium, in ch. xx., follows the second advent, and begins a visible kingdom of Christ on earth.

12. The Apocalypse, ch. iv.–xix., refers wholly to the times of the fourth or Roman empire.

13. The passage, xvii. 7–18, on the seven heads of the Beast, is one of direct interpretation; and its notes of time ought to be referred to the actual date of the prophecy, A.D. 96.

14. Babylon in the Apocalypse denotes Rome, or some power having its seat and centre at Rome.

15. The vision of the Seals, ch. iv., v., dates from the Ascension of our Lord.

[16. The first seal dates from the fall of Jerusalem, or nearly so.

17. The last vial coincides in time with the fall of Rome in its latest stage.]

18. The visions, ch. iv.–xvi., are included between the Ascension and the fall of Rome, except in their very close.

II.—*Structure.*

19. The Apocalypse is composed (ch. i. 19) of the things seen, ch. i., the things then present, ch. ii. iii., and the things to be hereafter, ch. iv.–xxii.

20. The last of these alone are direct prophecy, and were signified to the Apostle in visions by an angel, ch. i. 1, iv. 1, xxii. 8, 9.

21. The angelic visions are seven :—

(1) The seals, ch. v.–vii.

(2) The trumpets, viii.–xi.

(3) The woman and her seed, xii.–xiv.

(4) The vials, xv.–xvi.

(5) The fall of Babylon, xvii. 1–xix. 9.

(6) The Judgment, xix. 10–xxi. 8.

(7) The heavenly Jerusalem xxi. 9–xxii. 7.

22. The prophecy is successive from ch. xviii. to the close.

23. The ordinals in each sevenfold series are strictly successive in time.

24. The vision, ch. xii.–xiv., in its three parts is continuous and successive.

25. The events begin afresh after the seventh seal.

26. The passage, xi. 4–10, is a narrative parenthesis, and not a part of the *vision.*

27. The vision, x.—xi. 15, falls entirely within the sixth trumpet.

28. The three first visions close in common, in the time of the last vials.

29. They date from the opening of the prophecy, and are parallel.

30. The vials commence in the time of the seventh trumpet.

31. The sealing is successive, and reaches throughout the time of the trumpets.

32. The siege of Jericho is a divine type, and a full key to the structure.

III.—*General Application.*

33. The third woe is an open judgment on God's enemies, Babylon, the Beast, the False Prophet and the Dragon, ch. xviii.-xx.

34. The two first woes refer to the Saracens and the Turks.

35. The False Prophet is the same with the two-horned beast.

36. The beast throughout ch. xiii. refers to the eighth or revived headship.

37. The fourth beast, in Dan. vii., the body of the dragon, ch. xii., and the revived beast, ch. xiii., xvii., xi., are the rising Latin empire, the united Roman empire, and the revived Latin empire of the West.

38. The False Prophet is the same with the little horn, Dan. vii.

39. The False Prophet denotes the ecclesiastical Latin empire.

40. The Harlot, or Babylon in the stage of ch. xvii., is the same with the image of the beast.

41. Babylon denotes the Church defined by its seat on the seven hills of Rome.

42. The Woman denotes the Apostolic Church,

43. The sealed tribes denote Apostolic Christians throughout the times of the New Testament.

44. The palm-bearing multitude denotes the multitudes to be ingathered in the final triumph of the Church.

IV.—*Chronology*.

45. The number of the Beast, besides its other characters, is a mark of time and forms the transition from a mystical to the literal reckoning.

46. The time, times, and half a time, the 42 months, and 1260 days are the same interval.

47. The time, times, and a half of Daniel and the Revelation are the same period.

48. A prophetic day is a natural year.

49. The three-and-a-half times are the half of seven times, the whole season of Gentile power, and the same with the " latter times " of St. Paul.

[50. A time denotes 360 years, and χρόνος IS EQUIVALENT TO καιρός.]

The following axioms result simply from the combination of the previous principles.

51. The four first trumpets contain the judgments that fell on the Roman empire from the first century to the rise of the Saracens.

52. The third part denotes uniformly the third or Eastern empire; the fourth part, the fourth or Western empire.

53. The first trumpet relates to the fall of the Latin Emperorship of Rome.

54. The second trumpet relates to the Gothic irruptions before Constantine.

55. The third trumpet relates to the religious feuds of the East.

56. The fourth trumpet denotes the decline and long eclipse of the Eastern empire after Justinian.

57. The opening of ch. x. relates to the revival of learning and light after the fall of the Eastern empire at the Reformation.

58. The re-prophesying, and the resurrection of the witnesses both refer to the Reformation.

[59. The ascension of the witnesses relates to the era of missions.

60. The attendant earthquake is the first shock of the French Revolution.

61. The four first seals relate to four steps of imperial change, and four states of the visible Church: Apostolic, Nicene Orthodox, Superstitious and Papal, and the last in the climax of its corruption.

62. The fifth seal relates to the height of Papal power before the Reformation, and a time, χρόνος, intervenes before the sixth, while from the time of the oath, ch. x. 7, a *time* does not intervene.

63. The sixth seal begins with the French Revolution.]

64. The holding of the winds, ch. vii. 1, answers to the time since the general peace.

65. The harvest and vintage are still future and near at hand.

[66. The first four vials relate to the French Revolution.

67. The sixth vial is now accomplishing in Turkey and Christendom.

68. The seventh vial is near at hand.

69. The mystery of God will be accomplished within a time, or 360 years from the time of the Reformation.]

70. The seven epistles typically describe seven successive estates of the spiritual Church from the first to the second Advent.

V.—*Particular Times.*

71. The time, times and half, and 1260 days of Revelation are the same period.

72. The 42 months have a date rather later, like the two dates of the seventy years captivity.

73. The 1290 and 1335 days of Daniel both commence with the 1260 days of Revelation, or the time, times and a half of both prophecies.

[74. The seven times of the Gentiles begin with the subjection of Israel under Shalmanezer.

75. The three and a half times begin with Justinian's eternal code, A.D. 532–3.

76. The 42 months close nearly with the 1335 days.

77. The 42 months begin A.D. 604 or A.D. 607–8, with the reunion of the ten kingdoms or the public establishment of idolatry.

78. The 1335 days end in A.D. 1867–8.]"

The view of the structure, then, is one which I had maintained for twenty years as of primary importance, both in two writings of my own, and in eight successive editions of Mr. Bickersteth's work; an interval now enlarged to nearly forty years, without a single word of public retraction.

The statements of Mr. Elliott have now been circulating for seventeen years, without my being aware of their existence. He founds them on his own construc- *tion of a single* line in a private letter to him in 1856, which he quotes (vol. i., p. 549), not verbatim, but with his own comment, and misconstrues. The letter was clearly written with a friendly purpose of indicating any minor points in which I could honestly express approximation to his views. These were so secondary in my own view that I had quite forgotten having written it, and thus he himself treats all the points I specified with one exception. The words he quotes are these, " I agree with you now in the points following, the *Subordination* of the Trumpets to the Seals," to which he appends his own construction, " *i.e., that the seventh Seal is unfolded in the seven Trumpets.*" His view of my meaning is plainly disproved by his further quotations from the same letter. A structural "subordination" requires two conditions to be fulfilled ; that no part of the Seals belong to the fourteen centuries after the death of Theodosius, and none of the Trumpets to the four centuries before that date. The fourth and eighth points which I expressly re-affirmed in the letter quoted were, " The mystical sense of the sealed tribes, Rev. vii., as reaching through the whole dispensation ;" and that, " in the palm-bearing vision, Rev. vii., there is prospective reference to a time still future." As to the other point of the application of the earlier Trumpets, I re-affirmed my own view of the third and fourth parts in contrast to his. Vitringa, the leading advocate of the view I hold, expressly says, " As to the Trumpets, even if they are *subordinated* * to the Seals, according to the series of the prophetical context, nothing hinders them from commencing a new series of matters of a distinct argument ; this no skilful interpreter of the Book can deny, that the

* This very word appears to have been borrowed from Vitringa by me in my letter.

same is observed elsewhere in this very book, and everywhere in the prophecies."

It must seem strange that I should have left these statements so many years without contradiction. But the edition which contains them was published without any communication with me, either before or after publication, or any inquiry whether my words had been rightly interpreted.

I feel deep regret in having to utter this earnest protest, many years after the death of one whom I so much valued, and who has also expressed so warmly his sympathy and esteem as to two of my prophetical works. But I owe it both to myself, to the readers of my works, and of Mr. Bickersteth's "Practical Guide," emphatically to contradict these repeated statements.

In the quotation I have given from the "Practical Guide," I find now scarcely anything to alter in the ten pages on the structure, and the scheme at the close of the volume. In reprinting the axioms, I have put in small capitals the only point which I have renounced, and those in which I have made any modification are placed within brackets. I hold as strongly as ever that χρόνος denotes a definite period, but recognise now the truth of Mr. Elliott's dissent on one point; and that χρόνος does not denote the same period as καιρός.

My view of a double application (see pp. 10 and 12) by no means refers to the whole of the Apocalypse, which would involve evident absurdities; but, (1) to the first vision of the Seals, where the emblem is twofold of the horse and the rider, and Mr. Elliott's view of a fulfilment in successive stages of the degeneracy of the Roman State, from the peaceful state of the Antonines to the persecution of Diocletian, needs to be completed by the view which he so strongly rejects, of their application to the decline of the visible Church from its first purity to one of intense corruption and opposition to the truth, before the coming of Christ ; and, (2) to the vision of the Vials, the transition from the time of mystery to that of open manifestation, in which the mystical fulfilment will probably be succeeded by one closely resembling the plagues of Egypt, and fulfilling the prediction, Mic. vi. 15–17, in miraculous judgments on aggravated sin and blasphemy in the last days.

CHAPTER II.

The Calendar of Prophecy.

"The Approaching End of the Age," by Mr. Grattan Guinness, published in 1878, which has already reached a fifth edition, is a work worthy of most careful study by every thoughtful observer of the ways of Providence, and every sharer in the great hope of the Christian Church.

These are some of the great principles which the author ably unfolds :—

1st. "*Revelation of God in His works, and in His word, has been progressive in its character.* The Bible consists of sixty-three separate books, written by forty various authors, during a period of 1600 years. These develope a revelation which was continually unfolding itself through all those years, and close with a book bearing the Divine title of the 'Revelation of Jesus Christ.' . . . On no subject was full information given at the beginning; all was revealed in germ, and in the lapse of ages unfolded by degrees."

2nd. *Progressive Interpretation is a second main truth.*

"Human comprehension of Divine prophecy has been, and was intended to be, progressive."

The truth clearly unfolded by Mr. Guinness under this head, had been previously insisted upon at some length in my "Elements of Prophecy" (pp. 394–438).

3rd. *The world's history is a week of millennia.*

From the first century onward, the view has been widely

held that the seven days of creation have had and will have their counterpart in six millennia or work days of Divine Providence, to be followed by a seventh or sabbatic thousand years.

This view is inwrought into the Epistle of Barnabas in the first century, and into the apocryphal Book of Enoch in the second century. It has been held ever since by very many thoughtful writers.

This doctrine includes two main premises, first the truth of the Hebrew in contrast to the Septuagint chronology of the history of the Patriarchs. The Septuagint version introduced an ambiguity of 1500 years, foreshortening the Christian times to that extent, till the mist was fully removed by the actual delay of the time of judgment, from A.D. 500, to a time still future.

A second premiss is the commencement of human history with Adam about 4000 years before the Incarnation, to the exclusion of fictitious ages of Pre-historic man. Whether the unit of this great week is exactly 1000 solar years, or 1020, or 1040, or 1080, or 1050, for each of which some presumptions may be alleged, is a secondary detail.

4th. *The Bible contains a revealed system of times and seasons.* " Chronology is a prominent feature of the Holy Scriptures. In the account of the Creation, in the narrative of the Flood, in the biographies of the Patriarchs, in the Mosaic economy with its legal and ceremonial enactments, in the history of the Jewish nation, in the prophets, in the gospels, and in the Apocalypse, statements of time abound. Not only is the creation work recorded, but the time it occupied. Not only are the waters of the flood described, but we are told how many days they took to rise, and how many to fall; how many years Noah lived

E

prior to the crisis, how many days he waited before he
sent out the dove, and how many more before he went
forth from the ark himself."

"Unlike the sacred books of all false religions, Bible
stories are no vague myths or fabled occurrences, referred
to some remote, intangible past; the time of the events
is accurately measured, and they are fitted into a frame-
work of true chronology."

5th. *The Year-Day principle.* Mr. Guinness (pp. 304-
322) gives a clear and brief digest of my own arguments
for the Year-Day interpretation in the "Elements of
Prophecy" (pp. 308–414). Further reflection and later
study have confirmed and deepened my confidence in the
truths there stated, and have supplied me with some further arguments.

6th. *The Periodicity of Vital Phenomena* and the Law of
Completion in Weeks. Mr. Guinness has three chapters
on this subject (pp. 245–284), mainly original, and highly
interesting.

7th. *The data of the system of prophetic times,* as of
human chronology and calendars are four. The day, or
diurnal revolution of the earth; the week, or seven such
revolutions, or seven days. This is the primary type of
the whole scheme of Providence through 5000 years, and
is practically embodied in the history of creation. It is
inwrought into the scheme of Providence by the Jewish
or seventh-day Sabbath, through 4000 years to the
coming of Christ, and thenceforward by the Christian
Sabbath, the constant memorial of the resurrection of the
Lord on the first day of the week. The third element is
a year, or the time of the annual revolution of the earth in
its orbit. The fourth is the month, or the time of the
revolution of the moon in its orbit round the earth.

Now the three ratios, of the year to the day, of the month to the day, and the year to the month, are all incommensurable fractions. On the adjustment of these to each other by intercalation all the complexities of human calendars depend. The same causes enter still more profoundly into the system of sacred times ; the revelation of Him who is not only the "Alpha and Omega, the First and the Last," but Palmoni, "The Wonderful Numberer" (Dan. viii. 13), who "hath determined the times before appointed," as well as "made of one blood all nations of men to dwell on all the face of the earth."

Mr. Guinness brings out further the following relations, partly original, and in part derived from Mr. Cuninghame, M. de Cheseaux, and myself.

The adjustment of the four periods to each other has given birth to the following cycles, on which human calendars depend.

First, the Four-year Cycle, marked by the intercalation of one day in the fourth Julian year. This is the basis of the Julian and Gregorian calendars.

Secondly, the Twenty-eight-year Cycle, depending on the relation of the Julian year to the week, marked by the Sunday letters in the calendar.

Thirdly, the Nineteen-year Cycle, the Metonic Cycle of Ancient Greece, which harmonizes the year with the lunation, by an intercalation of seven months in nineteen years. This is marked by the golden number, and forms the basis of the Christian calendar both in the old and new style.

Fourthly, another relation is that of the Julian years in the Christian calendar to the lunar reckoning of the Mahometan calendar, a hundred of one being nearly equal to a hundred and three of the other, so that 1260 years of the Hegira form an interval of only 1222 years in the Christian calendar.

Fifthly, an Egyptian cycle of 25 years depends on the adjustment of the month to the Egyptian year of twelve months of thirty days, without the five additional days. Let A, B, C denote the fractions of a day, by which a year exceeds 365 days, by which the synodical month exceeds 29 days, and the sidereal month exceeds 27 days; we shall then have the following incommensurable ratios, giving birth when resolved into continued fractions, to different series of epacts or adjustments :—

$$1 : A$$
$$1 + A : 7$$
$$5 + A : 360$$
$$11 + A : 354$$
$$B : 1$$
$$6 + B : 7$$
$$1 + C : 7$$
$$365 + A : 29 + C$$
$$27 + B : 29 + C$$
$$365 + A : 27 + B$$
$$365 + A : 29 + C$$

There are thus eleven or twelve series of epacts, when these incommensurable ratios are solved by continued fractions. There are four others of a like kind, from other celestial periods; the precession of the equinoxes, the revolution of the nodes of the earth's orbit, the cycle of the eccentricity, and the cycle of the length of the seasons. To deduce any safe conclusion as to the relation of these to any particular integers, 6, 7, 5, 12, 8, and 13, all these series of epacts ought first to be *formed*, and then inductively compared together. But without this labour we may trace out in the sacred times of Scripture many features indicative of a divine plan.

Nineteen years is a fundamental cycle by which the solar year and the month are adjusted to each other.

315 years, one-fourth of 1260, is the next such period in order of accuracy. Forty-nine years, the period of the jubilee is a third such cycle. Forty-nine years equal just 606 lunations, so that from Nisan of the first year to Tizri of the fiftieth is just 600 lunations.

Two thousand three hundred years, or prophetic days, the period of Dan. viii. 14, is a luni-solar cycle of great accuracy in complete centuries.

One thousand and forty years, the excess of two thousand three hundred over 1260 years, is the most exact lunar cycle known. I have indicated this in my "Elements," pp. 368–372.

8th. Mr. Guinness insists with much force on the double relation of the sacred times to the solar and the lunar years. This is implied in the fundamental ordinance of creation (Gen. i. 1–18). We have its historical development in two great facts, that the solar year has been the basis of all Christian calendars for nineteen centuries, while the lunar year has been the basis of the Mahometan calendar for thirteen centuries, from the Hegira onward.

The period of seven times, or 2520 years, Mr. Guinness remarks, has a kind of natural primacy among numbers. Resolved into its factors it is—

$2^3 . 3^2 . 7 . 5$, or the continued product of the four first primes raised to the powers which give the greatest amount of factors. Thus the sum of the factors of 2520, including the number itself, is 9240. It is the most composite of all numbers, the sum of its factors being double itself + 1680.

The last number in Daniel, 1335 days, understood as years, is a time, times and a half, or 1260 years + 75 years. Now 75 is the exact epact, or the excess in the complete period of seven times, or 2520 years, of the number of the lunar years over the solar ; 2520 solar years being 2595 lunar years.

Mr. Guinness, I think, has been the first to give prominence to this remarkable relation. The idea of a twofold reckoning of the times, differing 75 years from each other, is common to many writers.

Another striking fact, which I have not seen noted before, is that from the era of Nabonassar, Feb. 26, B.C. 747, which, next to the era of the Olympiads, is the most fundamental date in profane chronology, to the deposition of Augustulus, Aug. 22, A.D. 476, the interval is exactly, to a day, 1260 lunar years, that is 1222 solar years, or a time, times and half a time in the lunar reckoning.

Another striking series of relations, is that of the great week of the world's history, 6000 years, followed by a seventh or sabbatic millennium. The jubilee of forty-nine years is 606 lunations, or 600 lunations to the jubilee month in the middle of the seventh sabbatic year.

The world before the Flood is parted from all later time by the 600 years of the life of Noah (Gen. vii. 6). "Noah was six hundred years old when the flood of waters was on the earth" (Gen. viii. 11, and viii. 13); or just one-tenth part of 6000 years.

I pass on to those parts of Mr. Guinness's work in which I either distrust his reasoning or dissent from his conclusions.

His Appendix A, of 200 pages, is the last of several attempts to establish a complete system of Bible chronology, partly on *à priori* grounds, which I have had to examine in the course of the last 33 years.

1. The first is that of Mr. Cuninghame in five successive works.

2. The second, Dr. Jarvis's "Chronological Enquiry into the History of the Church."

3. The third is Canon Browne's "Ordo Sæclorum."

4. The fourth is Greswell's Prolegomena, a Latin work of 400 pages in connection with his Dissertations.

Mr. Guinness's is the fifth.

Still, after all these labours, and partly from their conflict, the uncertainty in many minds seems rather to have increased than diminished. Thus Dr. Westcott seems to hold it doubtful. whether the crucifixion were on a Thursday or a Friday, and thinks that the fourth Gospel is at variance with the three others, both as to the week-day and month-day of the Passion. He thinks that its absolute date is still uncertain to the extent of 10 years, from A.D. 26 to A.D 36, and that it is uncertain whether the length of our Lord's public ministry were a little more than one year, or as much as ten. He even recommends the Church to rest content with this threefold uncertainty.

My reply to Canon Browne's pretended refutation of the Year-Day theory in the "Ordo Sæclorum," contains some cautions which apply alike to all the five systems. It was as follows :—

"Two opposite replies have been made to the argument from the seventy weeks for the Year-Day interpretation. Some deny the fact, and maintain that the seventy weeks denote weeks of *days*, and are still future.

Others deny the criticism. While they allow that the prophecy is fulfilled in years, they assert that its grammatical sense is merely seventy *sevens*, that is sevens of years, and that it contains no reference to days whatever. The two concessions, separately taken, are consistent with a rejection of the year-day theory; when combined together they concede the whole argument.

" Now in the ' Ordo Sæclorum,' *both these principles are conceded together*. The terms, grammatically, are held to have a reference to days, and a sort of literal fulfilment, but they are allowed to be fulfilled in years also. The following extract seems to be decisive of the author's view :—

" ' From this term (Sept., B.C. 459) we are to reckon $7 + 62 + \frac{1}{2}$ periods of seven years each. The first of these will terminate at B.C. 410, the second at B.C. 25, the third at the crucifixion, March, A.D. 29.' "

" ' In the chronography of our Lord's life, no date is more unanimously expressed by ancient authorities than Jan. 6th for His circumcision. Now, from this day to the Crucifixion are 437 days, and to the hour of the Passover $437\frac{1}{2} = 434 + 3\frac{1}{2}$, or sixty-two weeks and a half week, at the end of which half week Messiah is cut off. I cannot but therefore think that here we have a fulfilment of this memorable prophecy. . . . It may be that from the day and hour of Zechariah's vision to the instant of the circumcision, that great type of the cutting off of Messiah, is just the period of 62 weeks and a half week.' "

" It is not my purpose here to offer any opinion at length on the truth or solidity of these conclusions. One thing, however, is clear. If true, instead of demolishing the year-day theory, they confirm one main basis on which it rests. The analogy they would establish in its favour would be one of the strongest it is possible to conceive. The two contrasted lines of defence taken by its opponents are both swept away. The vision thus includes days in its proper meaning, so as to be twice fulfilled in days; and yet its main fulfilment is held to be in years. Those who hold the year-day principle, and yet look for a short triumph of infidelity at the last, could not frame an analogy more decisive in their favour than has been volunteered by our author; and this too, in the very system which was 'to have for one, and not the least important use, that it would help to demolish that vicious interpretation.'

"Canon Browne's scheme of chronology, then, in its real bearing on prophecy, illustrates once more the words of Thamus to Hermes in the allegory of Plato. 'O most ingenious Thoth, it is the part of one man to bring forth inventions, and of another to judge what effect they will produce. And you now, being parent of this invention, through parental prejudice have ascribed to it a power the exact opposite of the truth.'

"But while nothing can well be feebler or more inconclusive than the reasonings here advanced for these prophetical innovations, I would acknowledge freely the research and learning evinced by the author in the chronological inquiry. Still even here I conceive, a much more strict and cautious induction is needful, not only before infidels can be convinced, as the writer seems to hope, but before Christians themselves can yield to the evidence either of his or of any similar theory. The ways of God are in the deep waters. All things indeed are ordered in His counsel, in fixed times and seasons; and we may be sure that all His appointments are infinitely wise. But when we trace this counsel in the relation of

those times and seasons either to the properties of numbers or to the heavenly motions, we may soon get beyond
our depth, and confound illusions of our own fancy, or
even direct mistakes and false reasonings, with marks of
omniscient wisdom. So far as we follow the express teach-
ing of Scripture, we are safe. A little way beyond we may
perhaps venture, by the help of analogy to those truths
which are more clearly revealed. But the landmarks are
soon lost, when we enter on the tempting field of numerical speculation. Nowhere is the strictness of the Bacon-
ian philosophy, and the practical caution of Newton more
eminently needed. When we have been able to assign
an abstract reason why the year should be of the particular length 365·2422414 solar days, we may begin to
venture, without presumption, to form or to fortify a
system of chronology on abstract grounds. But if even
this first step very far transcends our abilities, we do well
to pause, before we dream of converting infidels, or think
of magnifying God's omniscient wisdom, by such a course
and order of investigation.

" It may be safely affirmed that, hitherto at least, to
attain certainty on the mere historic outlines of chronology
has been the utmost extent of real progress, and it may
well be doubted whether many have attained even thus far.
Let us take, for instance, that part of sacred chronology
which lies nearest ourselves, and where, if anywhere, we
might expect sure grounds of conviction. Three authors
have, quite of late, bestowed much pains on this subject :
Mr. Cuninghame, Mr. Greswell, and the writer of the
work here noticed. Three different years are assigned
by them to the Nativity, two to the Baptism of John,
three to our Lord's first Passover, and three to the Crucifixion. Besides these diversities, each is exposed to at

least one palpable objection when viewed as a complete system. Mr. Cuninghame's is based on a complete rejection, on very slender and insufficient grounds, of the main contemporary witness, Josephus, as wilfully dishonest and corrupt. Mr. Greswell's involves a hypothesis, demonstrably untrue, of an error in the week-day reckoning, in connection with the solar and lunar tables. Canon Browne's involves the entire rejection, against the judgment of all impartial critics, of two main notes of time in the gospel history, and the virtual contradiction of a third, besides other difficulties on which it is needless to dwell. While such is the present state of the sacred chronology in its most recent period, caution and reverence are eminently needed in those who address themselves to such inquiries. For assuredly the words of St. Paul apply with peculiar force to this vast and mysterious subject, the Divine ordination of times and seasons throughout all ages: 'Now we see through a glass, darkly; but then, face to face; now we know in part, but then shall we know even as we are known.' "—*The Four Prophetic Empires*, pp. 428–431.

I proceed to consider the main errors of the four systematic theories of *Cuninghame, Jarvis, Browne, and Greswell.*

Mr. Cuninghame, thirty-three years ago, in the five works named in Mr. Guinness's list, is the first in whom I have had to reject an *à priori* scheme or system of sacred chronology. His dogmatism is extreme, and my rejection of his conclusions brought on me severe censures.*

---

* Both Canon Browne and I were charged with "asinine stupidity." Dr. Benson, the candid and able ex-Master of the Temple, was said to have adopted a "happy expedient for avoiding the force of adverse testimony." I was said to be "guilty of no com-

The first principle was the arrangement of all the great eras of Providence at intervals of years which he called trinal fractions, which were not really fractions at all, but the doubles of the triangular numbers, increased by one. Such a law of Divine Providence is plainly most incredible and improbable in itself.

The other principles were these. First, the rejection of the Hebrew numbers, and the zealous advocacy of the Septuagint chronology as alone genuine. The second was the earnest advocacy of Usher's date of the Passion, A.D. 33, on the ground of its exact distance of seventy weeks complete from the seventh of Artaxerxes, B.C. 458. A third was the mathematical certainty of two rules for the celebration of the Passover. (1) That it must be after the true equinox. (2) That it must be on the very day of the true full moon. A fourth was a groundless charge against Josephus that his numbers were wilfully dishonest and corrupt. A fifth was the ascription to our Lord of a ministry of nearly four and a half years. I believed then, and believe now still more firmly, that every one of these principles was false and misleading.

The second à priori system is that of Mr. Greswell in his "Sacred Calendar," the Prolegomena to his valuable Dissertations on the Gospel History. The work professes to give the Jewish calendar year by year for seventeen centuries, from the Exodus to the close of the Canon, but it is vitiated throughout by a strange error, well exposed by Canon Browne in the "Ordo Sæclorum" (pp. 510–545). The error is the hypothesis of an inter-

mon blunder and defiance and contempt for all authentic records of Jewish times," and of "sophistry in argument hateful to God." —See *Churchman's Monthly Review*, 1847, art. on "Cuninghame *on* the True Date of the Passion."

ruption of two days in the weekly cycle, between the Council of Nice and the Gregorian calendar. This would really imply that a defective week of five days only, had occurred somewhere in that interval, without the least notice of it by either Christian or profane writers. This is plainly impossible, and the whole work is changed by it into a series of laborious ambiguities. Mr. Browne says, " If these absurdities had appeared in the pages of a writer of inferior note, I should not have gone at such length into the refutation of them. It really is high time, for the credit of our age in such matters, that so glaring a blemish should be exposed; since the question is one of arithmetic and common sense, I may without arrogance affirm that the refutation is complete. The hypothesis is simply futile with respect to the purpose for which it was started, and is tenable in no sense and for no purpose whatever." With this censure I fully agree, though Mr. Greswell is a writer to whom I feel more indebted than any other on the general subject, and Mr. Browne's work, as a whole, I think very inferior to his Dissertations.

A third systematic work on Gospel Chronology of high pretension, is that of Dr. Jarvis, the historiographer of the American Episcopal Church. His work of 400 pages contains a large amount of chronological materials, and lays down in the Preface some very sound principles. " No theory before examination is to be assumed; testimony is to be followed wheresoever it may lead. The two great objects constantly kept in view must be the investigation of truth for its own sake, and the lucid communication of that truth to others. In the examination of testimony the original author is, if possible, to be consulted; a fruitful source of error is

copying authorities from the works of modern writers
on chronology. Each brings forward such testimony as
he thinks adapted to sustain his point. They are special
pleaders arguing a case; all they say is to be duly
weighed, but the judge notes down the authorities they
offer, and then examines them for himself."

These sound principles, and much valuable matter on
the Olympiads, the Roman year, the Date of Censorinus,
and the series of the Emperors and Consuls, are rendered
almost nugatory by one strange mistake. Professing to
correct a mistake in all previous chronologers, by which,
he says, the whole consular chronology for 200 years, from
the time of Julius Cæsar to the reign of Antoninus has
been thrown into disorder, he himself commits the very
error which he wrongly charges on them. He counts
twice over the year A.D. 161, because the consuls of that
year, being the two Augusti, were often recorded in the
consular lists under that title. He thus deranges all the
dates from Julius Cæsar to Commodus by one year, and
vitiates all his own reasonings on the Gospel chronology
in connection with the paschal cycles.

Canon Browne's "Ordo Sæclorum" (a work of 700
pages), the fourth systematic work, which I have ex-
amined, contains, like that of Dr. Jarvis, a great deal of
research and valuable chronological material. Its ex-
posure of the error of Mr. Greswell in his Calendar, is
very clear and decisive; but the work itself is almost a
chaos of learned conjecture. It includes: (1) An attempt
to restore the Assyrian, Babylonian and Egyptian chrono-
logies from Manetho and Berosus, with hardly any reference to modern researches; (2) A Harmony of the Four
Gospels, of which the first principle is that St. Matthew's
Gospel is a translation of an Aramaic original, in which

the translator has confused with each other two or three different Galilean circuits of Christ.

The author begins his attempt to construct a Gospel chronology by altering conjecturally two of the main data, Luke vi. 1; John vi. 4. Its chief feature is a revival of the view of the early Valentinians so strongly denounced by Irenæus, which confined the ministry of Christ to a single year. This is flatly opposed to the constant view of the Church for eighteen centuries, and to a dozen direct or indirect indications in the Gospels. What Dr. Westcott strangely calls a " strong case," is made up of a series of violent and almost impossible conjectures.

(3) Canon Browne's next principle is a rejection of the view of the Four Empires, as held by the Church from the beginning, on the faith of the superficial objections of Mr. Maitland, the emptiness of which I have elsewhere exposed.

(4) We have next an Exposition of the Apocalypse, of which the basis is an assumption of its Neronic date, the utter baselessness of which is proved alike by the external and internal evidence, and has been afresh demonstrated by Mr. Elliott. And its second main feature is the degradation of the inspired prophecy into a mere endorsement by the Holy Spirit of a false impression of some early Christians that Nero would rise from the dead, and be the last Antichrist. This profane fancy, which turns the crowning message of God to the Church into a false prophecy, is the sum of the twenty pages which Canon Browne has given to this topic.

(5) A fifth principle laid down (p. 24) is that the year-day principle is a " mere fiction invented by heretics, and since adopted chiefly as a weapon of controversy."

His convincing proof of this consists of two assumptions with regard to the seventy weeks, which, if they were demonstrated truths, instead of being in part conjectural like the rest of the book, would prove the exact reverse, and establish, in that case, the theory he seeks to overthrow.

His two sections on the chronology of the Acts and on the dates of the three first Gospels, seem to me a nearer approach to the truth than the rest of his work.

Mr. Guinness's book, in care and accuracy, is a refreshing contrast to the errors, and the special or general inaccuracies of the four systems I have named. But my experience of these makes me dissatisfied with regard to one main principle involved in Appendix A, in which he would settle dates in part by reference to the numerical properties of what he calls the lunar epacts. Such evidence could only be safely admitted after an inductive search into the terms of twenty or thirty distinct series, when the incommensurable ratios of different chronological units have all been resolved into continued fractions.

It seems to me very doubtful whether much of the specialty on which Mr. Guinness founds this part of his theory, is not due to a partial selection, unconsciously made, of *some* epact numbers out of many; and that the special relations of the epacts to the numbers 6, 7, 8, 13, would probably disappear on a comprehensive examination of *all* the epact numbers.

Yet his remarks certainly include many elements which are both true and deeply suggestive.

I would conclude with mentioning two points, one doctrinal and one chronological, in which I think an important correction is needed.

First, in pp. 54–78, many great and solemn truths as

to the Millennium, the Resurrection and the Judgment
are clearly stated; but these are mingled, I conceive,
with one great and serious error of primary importance.
I agree fully with the first main principle, that the resurrection of the dead and the judgment to come, are
revealed as to be accomplished in two successive stages.
The contrast of character and issue is made still more
striking by this contrast of time. But Mr. Guinness, if I
understand him aright, conjoins with this exposition two
other statements which I believe to be wholly contrary to
Scripture. (1) That the judgment in Rev. xx. is not the
same with, but wholly different from, the judgment in
Matt. xxv. (2) That the judgment in Rev. xx. is of the
unfaithful dead only, and that the faithful, or the Church
of the First Resurrection, never come into judgment at
all. For this I see no ground but Alford's altered translation of John v. 24, which I believe to be a mistake. The
words of Rev. xi. 17, 18, distinctly refer to the same
event as chap. xx. They define it as "a time of the
dead that they should be judged," including the faithful
and the unfaithful dead alike, the faithful being here specified—" That Thou shouldest give reward to Thy servants
the prophets, and to the saints, and to them that fear
Thy name, small and great, and shouldest destroy them
that destroy the earth." In the other chapter (xx.) the
expression, "*the rest of the dead* lived not till the thousand years were ended," shows just as plainly that the
heirs of the first resurrection, whose blessing is first
described, are included among the dead whose "time"
in this vision has then "come to be judged," though with
a total contrast in the issue of the judgment, and a distinction also in the record of the resurrection.

The thousand years are the great Millennial Day. The

faithful are to be raised in the morning of that day; the unfaithful not till its close. The first step in the acquittal of the righteous and the condemnation of the unrighteous is simultaneous. So our Lord says, Matt. xvi. 27, " The Son of man shall come in the glory of His Father, with the holy angels, and then shall He reward every man according to his works." So in 2 Cor. v. 10, " We must all appear before the judgment seat of Christ, that every man may receive the things done in his body according to that he hath done, whether it be good or bad."

And the Lord Himself in His parting message, " Behold I come quickly, and My reward is with Me, to give to every man according as his work shall be. I, Jesus, have sent Mine angel to testify these things in the churches."

Three truths are revealed with equal plainness. First, that the judgment includes all mankind, for God is "the Judge of all" (Heb. xii. 23). Secondly, that this judgment is by Christ, the incarnate and exalted Saviour. " The Father judgeth no man, but hath committed all judgment unto the Son, because He is the Son of man." Thirdly, that it includes two classes, contrasted alike in their character and in the issue of the judgment; described in Rev. xx. as the children of the first resurrection, and "the rest of the dead," both alike dead when this day of judgment begins; and in Matt. xxv. as the sheep who are placed at the right hand, and the goats who are placed at the left.

To teach that the righteous are to be exempted from judgment, because of the greatness of the honour bestowed on them at the first resurrection, really involves a contradiction of a cardinal truth of Scripture, and contains the germ of the worst antinomianism. The Church of the Firstborn, the Bride, the Children of the Resurrection, in claiming exemption from this revealed purpose of God, would be guilty of high treason against the King of kings.

It is so far from being the case that the Bride is exempt from judgment, that the Lord Himself, the Son of God only reassumed the glory He laid aside for our redemption as the signet and ratification of a public judgment of God the Father on the perfection of His finished work. John xvii. 4, 5, "I have glorified Thee on the earth, I have finished the work which Thou gavest Me to do: and now, O Father, glorify Thou Me with the glory which I had with Thee before the world was." His resurrection was a formal ratification of this great truth.

II. The chronological question refers to the two fundamental dates of the Nativity and the Crucifixion. For the Nativity Mr. Guinness adopts the date of Lewin alone, August, B.C. 6, and for the Crucifixion that of Benson and Clinton, A.D. 29, rejecting that of Greswell, Alford, Wordsworth, Wieseler, Ellicott, Thompson, McClellan and myself.

Thus, in my view and that of the above writers he antedates the Nativity 15 months and the Crucifixion a year, thus increasing the interval by three months. His proposed aim is to show that our Lord's earthly life was exactly 33 years 7 months and 7 days, which he calls a soli-lunar cycle, in which time the sun gains on the moon one solar year.

Now first that precise interval is not a cycle at all; for the essence of a cycle is the coincidence of an integer with an integer period, as of 19 years with 235 months. But the period in question includes a fraction of a year, a fraction of a month, and even of a day. If the lunar recession is compared with a sidereal year, the period would be 33 years 5 months and 1 day or fraction of a day; if with the tropical year, 33 years 6 months and 15 days. Either of these is very near to the much simpler relation of one-third of a century, or 33 years and 4 months.

He rightly takes the Nativity, not the Annunciation, as the commencement of our Lord's earthly life, but to be consistent with his own reasoning (p. 553) he ought to date it from the Annunciation. He says there on a kindred subject, "If normal human existence were only seventy years, as it is popularly considered, instead of what it is accurately, between nine and ten months more, dated from conception its true commencement, this accurate coincidence would entirely disappear." I think the proper limits of our Lord's earthly life are certainly the Nativity and the Resurrection; the forty days after the Resurrection are plainly unlike in kind, but Mr. Guinness includes these forty days to make up his supposed cycle.

The question of a year earlier or later, that is from B.C. 6—A.D. 29, or from B.C. 5—A.D. 30, leaving the interval the same, can be rightly decided only by a careful historical investigation of the Passover Days and the Courses of the Priests. I have made this investigation, and hope shortly to publish it in a work on the "Historical Basis of the Gospels." My view, in which both events are placed one year later, fully satisfies whatever is sound in Mr. Guinness's own theory. My conclusion is that the earthly life of our Lord was 33 solar years and 4 months, or 34 lunar years and 4 months. Now this is the unit which harmonizes the Christian and the Mahometan calendars, because 103 lunar years are 100 solar years.

Thus a slight correction of Mr. Guinness's hypothesis as to the exact date of the Nativity and Resurrection, only confirms and redoubles the evidence for the general principle, and frees it from some details that disguise and obscure the simplicity of the main idea.

CHAPTER III.

THE Apostle St. Peter describes the word of prophecy by a solemn and instructive emblem, as " a light that shineth in a dark place." The present world, we are thus taught, and experience confirms the truth, is like a troubled and trackless ocean. It is a place which sin has filled with confusion, and buried in gloom. Its history is one perpetual round of strife, and war, and tumultuous violence. Empires may rise and perish; generations may come and pass away; but the confusion is still the same. The children of the world walk on still in darkness. The mystery and the gloom are as deep as ever; and while the Christian gazes thoughfully on the scene, the inquiry of the prophet rises to his lips, " O my Lord, what shall be the end of these things ? "

But the word of prophecy is a bright and cheering lamp amid the world's darkness. There, in those sacred pages we behold a scheme of redemption which is from everlasting to everlasting, but which is daily unfolding itself in the history of our fallen world. There we learn that however the counsels of man may fail, though empires may perish and generations may pass away, there is a counsel that shall stand for ever, and a kingdom that cannot be destroyed,—the counsel of God, and the kingdom of the Most High. The mist and darkness are rolled away from the landscape of Divine Providence, and *we can trace* from age to age the unveiling of God's

infinite goodness, in the recovery of our guilty race to the
presence of His holiness, and the enjoyment of His love.
The dispensations of His grace present themselves in succession to our view; and still, as they advance, increase
in their clearness and beauty, till at length the triumph
of a Saviour's mercy is complete, and "the kingdoms of
this world become the kingdoms of our Lord." Thus
the word of prophecy when received in simple faith, ful-
fils its appointed office as a beacon-light, and leads our
thoughts onward through all the changes of time, to that
"rest which remaineth for the people of God."

Light then, and not darkness, is the true character of
all the inspired prophecies. But the description applies
most fully to those which predict the past desolation and
future glory of Israel. The visions of Daniel and St.
John retain an air of mystery that accords well with their
reference to the Gentile dispensation, that time which is
called emphatically, *the mystery of God.* But the prophecies
which relate to the Jews are free from this symbolical
veil. They are clothed in simple language; they stoop
to our earthly estate; they are imbedded in the facts of
history, and confirmed by visible earnests of their truth.
To the spiritual and sanctifying power which they share
with all the Divine promises, they add the intense reality
of persons, and scenes, and places, which are within our
reach, or even before our eyes. The stronghold of man's
unbelief lies in the things which are seen and temporal.
But these prophecies assail it even here. They reveal to
us a counsel of God plainly fulfilling itself on the face of
the earth. They show us a country marked off, a people
separated, as visible witnesses, first of His just severity
against sin, and then of His overflowing mercy and
unchangeable goodness. The spell of Infidelity is thus

broken, which would keep our earth separate from heaven; and the golden links are seen already in being, which will shortly bind them together in perfect union. With a variety and fulness of truth, which opens a boundless field for hope, meditation, and prayer, there is in these predictions a simplicity which the meanest Christian may understand. The promise of God tempers itself to our feeble vision, and by a vision of the blessedness of the earthly Jerusalem prepares the eyes of Christians for the higher and fuller glory of the Jerusalem above.

When we turn from this view of prophecy to the actual state of the Church, how painful is the contrast! The light shines in the darkness, but the darkness receives it not. The lamp which God has vouchsafed to us for our guidance is neglected or even scorned, by the great body of those who bear the name of Christians. The calculations of their own worldly prudence eclipse the messages of the Infinite Wisdom. They boldly reverse the commandment of the Holy Ghost. While He charges us to take heed to the word of prophecy, they brand attention to it as enthusiastic folly, or the dreams of madness. Nay many, even of the followers of Christ, are entangled though to a less degree, in the same grievous snare, and practically discourage that which the Spirit of God so earnestly commends. So that a part of the inspired oracles, nearly as large as the whole of the New Testament, comes to be entirely neglected; or else furnishes, at most, only a few vague hopes and general lessons of warning; while its main purpose is overlooked, and the rich variety of Divine truth which it contains is uncared for and unexplored.

To what cause must we ascribe this neglect of Old *Testament* prophecy, which has been till of late, and we fear still continues to be so marked a feature of the Gentile Church ?   In the great body of nominal Christians it arises, doubtless, from man's natural aversion to the Word of God, and his dislike to realize the presence of his Maker.   Its source, in more spiritual Christians, is the selfishness which clings even to the regenerate soul, and which struggles mightily against the power of Divine grace.   In the unbeliever this selfishness reigns and triumphs ; but where the work of faith is begun, the enemy puts on a spiritual garb, and tutors the soul to be selfish in the things of God.   Personal safety is then placed higher than the glory of the Saviour.   The question becomes, how low a stage of grace will secure from danger, not how largely may Christ be honoured and served.   How little truth is sufficient and essential, not how much may we hope to receive, and how much is the God of all grace willing to bestow.   And since the effect of the Jewish prophecies on personal edification is less self-evident than in some other parts of scripture, we doubt the wisdom of God, who pronounces every part to be profitable for our instruction in righteousness ; and we thus remain under the blight of a spiritual selfishness, that withers and deadens all the strength of the soul.

But there is a further cause of this general neglect, in the wide-spread feeling of uncertainty and doubt as to the true sense of the Scripture prophecies.   Many things have concurred to this effect ; the mysteriousness which must be admitted, in some few of the prophecies them-selves, the variations of numerous expositors, the gross perversions of some, the vague, uncertain allegories of others, and the currency of the false maxim, that all predictions when fulfilled are clear, and when unfulfilled, obscure and inexplicable.   These causes and such as these, have changed the faith of multitudes in the Church into bewildering uncertainty. The vision, according to God's own warning, has become " as the words of a book that is sealed " (Isa. xxix. 11). Divines have maintained, in the face of the clearest examples and plainest warnings, that the inspired predictions were not meant to be understood till after their fulfilment. So that the metaphor of the apostle has been actually reversed. Christians have come to describe the word of prophecy, not as the beacon-light, but as a trackless and dangerous ocean. They have thus ventured to be wise above what is written, and have warned their brethren against that very study on which the Holy Spirit has pronounced a solemn and repeated blessing.

What then, in this state of the Church, is the duty of Christ's ministers, the appointed stewards of the mysteries of God ? The words of the prophet (Hab. ii. 1, 2) supply us with an answer. He had just given the Jews warning of the Chaldean invasion. The Spirit of God taught him that however plainly the message was given, they "would in no wise believe it." He prepares himself for sceptical doubts and contentious opposition. He seeks for wisdom from above. " I will stand upon my watch, and set me on my tower, and watch what He will say unto me, and what I shall answer when I am argued with." And he receives a gracious answer. He is to write the message in clear characters, and expose it on tablets to the public view, that even the most careless might have no excuse for ignorance. " The Lord answered and said unto me, Write the vision, and make it plain upon tablets, that he may run that readeth it."

The spirit of this command applies clearly to min-*isters of Christ* in the present day. The importance of a knowledge of God's prophecies to the Church has not ceased, and cannot cease, till her Lord's return. The prophecy teaches this in the very next verse as explained by St. Paul. " The vision," we are told, " is for an appointed time," even " until He that shall come will come, and He will not tarry " (Hab. ii. 3 ; Heb. x. 37). Till then the same duty rests on His messengers. Since the word of prophecy has been covered with the mist of false glosses, or cankered by the rust of neglect, they must clear away the doubts that obscure it, and restore the engraving in fuller and broader relief ; and so present it to a careless world with the stamp of God's veracity, and the bright and clear impress of heavenly and everlasting truth.

To fulfil this command, in humble dependence on the blessing of God, is my present aim. My object is to make the vision plain, as on tablets, to the most casual observer ; and with this view, I would first explain what is meant by the literal interpretation of Old Testament prophecy, and then confirm it by scriptural arguments.

What then is the literal sense of prophecy ? False notions on this point have been very general. Absurd consequences have been grafted upon these, in order to justify a system of glosses and allegories, and to transfer all the Jewish promises to the Gentile Church. The definition may be given in two forms, which agree in their result, and help to explain each other. First, the literal sense is that in which we adhere to the common usage of terms, and the natural scope of the passage as inferred from the context alone. Secondly, it is when we attach to a prophecy the same sense which we should naturally assign to it if it were a history of past events, and not a prediction of things future.

I will explain by a few examples. The prophet Isaiah, in chap. iv., has the following words : " And it shall come to pass, that he that is left in Zion, and he that remaineth in Jerusalem, shall be called holy, even every one that is written among the living in Jerusalem : When the Lord shall have washed away the filth of the daughters of Zion, and shall have purged the blood of Jerusalem from the midst thereof by the spirit of judgment, and the spirit of burning. And the Lord shall create upon every dwelling-place of Mount Zion, and upon all her assemblies, a cloud and a smoke by day, and the shining of a flaming fire by night, for upon all the glory shall be a defence." (Isa. iv. 5.)

Here the context determines the literal meaning. The Jerusalem spoken of is the same of which it was said just before, " Jerusalem is ruined, and Judah is fallen ; because their tongue and their doings are against the Lord to provoke the eyes of His glory " (Isa. iii. 8). The daughters of Zion are the same class who have just been so sternly reproved for their haughtiness and pride, the daughters of Israel dwelling at Jerusalem. The assemblies of Mount Zion are the same of which it has been declared, " The calling of assemblies I cannot away with: it is iniquity, even the solemn meeting : " (Isa. i. 13) they are the assemblies of Israel for worship in the holy city. The literal sense is, therefore, that Jerusalem then fallen so low should rise from her ruin ; that her daughters should be as glorious for purity and meekness as once they were detestable for their pride ; that the judgments of God, and the power of His Spirit, shall effect this mighty change ; that all the dwellers in Jerusalem shall then be holy, without any mixture of the *profane;* and that a glory, like the pillar of cloud and of fire in the desert, shall then rest, as a sacred token of God's holy presence, upon all the assemblies for solemn worship in Jerusalem.

Again, let us compare Isa. i. 7–10 with the opening of chap. lxii., and, on applying the second definition, the sense of the prophecy will be clear. One passage is historical, the other prophetic; one speaks of Zion's glory, the other of her shame; but in other respects they entirely correspond. If we expound the prophecy as the history must be expounded, no doubt can arise upon its meaning. The country which is to receive the name of Beulah, in token of God's peculiar favour, is the same which before had been " desolate and burned with fire " (Isa. i. 7), the land of Israel. The daughter of Zion, to whom the high surname is to be given, Hephzibah, " My delight is in her," the Zion for whose brightness and salvation Messiah pleads with unceasing fervour, is the same that was left " as a cottage in a vineyard, and as a besieged city," while the Assyrian invaders were overspreading the land. The figures used in the second place to express the glory of Zion are scarcely stronger than those in the first to express her degradation. Is it said, in imagery of striking beauty, " Thou shalt be a crown of glory in the hand of the Lord, and a royal diadem in the hand of thy God ? " A metaphor not less vivid has been used to describe her corruption : " Hear the word of the Lord, ye rulers of Sodom ; give ear to the law of our God, ye people of Gomorrah." The same laws of thought by which we interpret the history, enable us without any further strain upon language, or recourse to allegories, to expound the prophecy also.

But there are three main difficulties which have perplexed this subject, and which I must endeavour to remove. These are, the presence of FIGURATIVE TERMS, the SYMBOLICAL nature of some of the PROPHECIES, and the ANALOGICAL or TYPICAL APPLICATIONS of others. The definition of the literal sense which has been already given will furnish us, in every case, with an easy solution.

First, it has often been thought that to advocate the literal sense of prophecy involves the absurd consequence of denying all metaphorical and figurative language. And the strange paradoxes which must be maintained on this view are sometimes urged with an air of triumph, to prove the need for adopting allegorical glosses, and rejecting the literal sense. Specimens of such paradoxes might be multiplied with ease, if it were consistent with due reverence for God's most holy Word. But to all such objections, whether brought forward with flippancy or with seriousness, there is a simple reply. The literal interpretation, rightly understood, does not exclude the admission of figures "wherever the context of itself shows their presence, or wherever we should allow them to exist, if the prophecy were a history of past events."

How beautiful, for instance, is the patriarch's blessing upon his favoured son !   " Joseph is a fruitful bough, a fruitful bough by a well, whose branches run over the wall : the archers have sorely grieved him, and shot at him, and hated him : but his bow abode in strength, and the arms of his hands were made strong by the hands of the mighty God of Jacob." (Gen. xlix. 22–24.) Let us compare this with the close of the blessing of Moses on the tribe of Joseph. " His glory is as the firstling of his bullock, and his horns are as the horns of unicorns ; with them shall he push the people to the ends of the earth ; and they are the ten thousands of Ephraim, and the thousands of Manasseh " Deut. xxxiii. 17).   In the first, or historical passage, we find it easy to expound the figures, and still to retain their literal application to the sufferings of Joseph and the treachery of his brethren. Why, then, should the metaphors in the words of Moses obscure from us its literal application to the tribe of Joseph? Or why, because of the presence of figures, should we have recourse to systematic allegory in prophecies of the future more than in histories of the past? The metaphors, in each case, are only a veil beneath which the literal sense is preserved transparent and entire.

THE SYMBOLICAL PROPHECIES, again, have perplexed the minds of many Christians, and obscured from them the evidence for the literal interpretation of the rest. The visions of Daniel and the Apocalypse cannot, it is argued, be taken literally, without gross and glaring absurdity. We cannot suppose that locusts with stings like scorpions are literally to arise out of the abyss, or that a woman literally clothed with the sun has ever appeared, or will appear. Since, then, in these emblems, and many besides, such an interpretation would be absurd, why should we affix a literal meaning to the other prophecies?

But here, too, the difficulty melts away upon a close inspection. For, in truth, in these parts of the word of God we have not a direct and literal prophecy of the future, but only the literal record of a past vision. The Spirit of God makes use of symbols, addressed to the eye and ear of the prophet, as a peculiar language, more adapted than that in common use to convey to us the prediction in the comprehensive fulness of its meaning. We have first of all then, by a literal interpretation, to realize the scenes and objects of the vision; and those scenes themselves then furnish a kind of natural language, which leads simply to the true sense of the prophecy. A literal interpretation is not excluded by the presence of symbols; it is rather implied as the basis and groundwork of their correct exposition. The *record* must be strictly and literally interpreted, before the *vision* can be explained in its full symbolic meaning.

There are, it is true, mingled with these visions, passages directly prophetic, given us by the Holy Spirit as further helps in deciphering the mysterious language of those symbols which he employs. To these, accordingly, the rule of literal interpretation fully applies. The latter part of Dan. ii., vii., viii., the whole of Rev. xvii., and some verses in the other chapters, are of this kind. But the peculiar nature of the context leads, in this case, to a slight modification, the nature and reason of which a few words may explain.

If these passages were independent predictions, they ought, for their literal exposition, to be explained just as if they were histories of past events, written in the common language of men. But since they are given as helps to ascertain the meaning of the previous visions, there will be, as in the material world, a kind of reaction upon their own meaning, from the nature of the visions to be explained. The Holy Spirit here employs a double medium of prophecy—the symbolic language of the vision itself, and the common language of the explanatory supplement. The bare fact that both are employed, implies that either would be imperfect if taken alone. The sense, therefore, of each, when doubtful, ought to be fixed by the light which the other supplies. Just as we are to assign that significance to the emblems, which agrees best with the Divine explanation; so, where the *explanation* itself contains peculiar or ambiguous terms, that meaning ought to be given them which harmonizes best with the Divine emblems. The law of literal interpretation still holds true; the circumstances of its application alone have varied. The symbolic prophecies, far from impeaching its truth, present it in a fresh light, and yield it fuller confirmation.

A third ground of objection or difficulty, has been the FIGURATIVE APPLICATIONS OF PROPHECY IN THE NEW TESTAMENT. Some instances of these clearly exist, though much fewer than is often supposed. Whether we admit or reject the literal sense of Malachi's prediction concerning Elijah (Mal. iv. 5), or that in Hosea of the restoration of the ten tribes (Hos. i. 10; ii. 23), it is plain that our Lord applies the first of these to the Baptist (Matt. xi. 14), and that St. Paul quotes the second in connexion with the call of the Gentiles (Rom. ix. 24–26). Have we not, then, a sufficient ground for rejecting the literal sense, not only in these passages, but in all those which seem to predict a future glory of Israel?

The fallacy of such a conclusion will be seen by comparing these applications of prophecy with the types in the narrative portions of Scripture. We know, on the authority of St. Paul (Gal. iv. 24), that the history of Hagar and Sarah, of Ishmael and Isaac, is to be viewed as a Divine allegory of the two covenants. But what sound interpreter would dream of denying, on this account, the historical truth of that sacred narrative? In the prophet Hosea, again (xi. 1), the Lord reminds His people of His mercy to them in their first exodus: "When Israel was a child, then I loved him, and called my son out of Egypt." The Evangelist, however (Matt. ii. 15), teaches us to read in this a prophecy of our Saviour's flight into Egypt and of his return to Judea.

G

Yet no one has ever fancied this to be any presumption against the historical certainty of that first exodus of Israel. The rest of Canaan, as the apostle teaches the Hebrew Christians (Heb. iv.), was a shadow and earnest of the true rest which remaineth for God's people. But the entrance of the Jews under Joshua into Canaan is not the less a plain fact of sacred history. What reason have we to adopt a different rule in the case of inspired prophecies? These are only history written before the event, and the analogical lessons that are entwined with them form no presumption against their literal truth. The events recorded in the books of Genesis and Joshua are undoubted facts, though we have inspired warrant for asserting their typical meaning. Why, then, should we doubt the reality of the future glories of Israel, because they form such expressive emblems of spiritual and heavenly things?

The literal interpretation, therefore, when rightly understood, admits of an intermixture of figurative language, is the true groundwork of symbolic exposition; and consistent with allegorical applications, wherever they can be proved from Scripture itself, and are not perverted, so as to set aside the direct meaning of the prophecy. Let us now proceed, in the second place, TO ESTABLISH ITS TRUTH BY SOME SCRIPTURAL ARGUMENTS.

The first of these we may draw from the words of God to Habakkuk. The command of God is there given to the prophet, "Write the vision, and make it plain upon tables, that he may run that readeth it." We may here adopt the reasoning of our blessed Lord, "Is not the life more than meat, and the body than raiment?" (Matt. vi. 25.) As the goodness of God enables us from the *greater gift* to infer the less, so His wisdom warrants us to infer, where the less is promised, that the greater, without which it would be useless, has already been given. Is it not, then, more important to the Church, that the language of prophecy should be simple, than that its written characters should be large and plain? Would it not be like a mockery, first to clothe it in allegories, the meaning of which no reader, at that time, could possibly divine, and then to charge the prophet about the public manner of its exhibition, or the distinctness of the engraving? Surely these words are of themselves a convincing proof, that the language of God's prophecies, where not expressly sealed, is intelligible and plain; that the only veil is the blindness of our own eyes, and the only seal upon the vision our negligence or unbelief.

Another argument we may gather from the form of the Jewish prophecies, and the manner of their communication. They are publicly addressed to the Jews themselves. They relate to objects and scenes with which they were familiar. They are given as pledges of the Divine goodness, in contrast with their own sin and degradation. They are attended with the charge, even to the carnal Israelites, in various forms—"Believe the prophets of God, and ye shall prosper." They are intermingled with the actual history of that very people, whose future dignity and glory they seem to announce so clearly. They are worded as if to exclude the very possibility of turning them from their natural meaning. " Jerusalem shall be inhabited in her own place, even in Jerusalem." (Zech. xii. 6.) The Jews are to be " gathered into their own land, and none of them left any more at all " among the heathen (Ezek. xxxix. 28). If God's covenant with day and night should fail, then only shall Israel cease to

be a nation before him.   (Jer. xxxiii. 25, 26.)   Distinct
promises are made to the holy city, to the chosen people,
and to the very mountains of Israel.   The land that has
been "taken up in the lips of talkers" (how striking a
description even now!) "shall bear the reproach of the
people no more," and "bereave its dwellers no more," but
"shoot forth its branches for the people of Israel, who
are at hand to come." (See Ezek. xxxvi.)   Who can
read such passages, and not feel that the Spirit of God
has hedged round His predictions with a sacred fence
against every attempt to distort them from their simple
and literal meaning ?

The conduct of the apostles, and the reproofs addressed
to them by our Lord, are a further evidence of the same
truth.   Many times are they reproved for not receiving
a prophecy in its literal sense, never once for so receiving
it.   They plainly understood the promises made to Israel
in this literal manner, but for this our Lord never blames
them.   His censures are all aimed against their unbelief
of other statements, equally plain, of Messiah's sufferings.
Such was the rebuke on the way to Emmaus, "O fools,
and slow of heart to believe all that the prophets have
spoken." (Luke xxiv. 25.)   However chargeable with
dulness in other respects, here they are not charged with
being dull to understand, but slow to *believe*.   It was
with them as with Christians now.   Some sayings of the
prophets pleased their taste, or tallied with their system,
but others were of an opposite kind.   They chose out,
therefore, which they would believe, and tropes and
figures served them doubtless to explain the rest.

A fourth and most convincing argument for the literal
interpretation may be found in the past history of the
Jews.   The ...tings pronounced against them have

been strictly fulfilled; then so must the promises be also. Out of many examples, let us choose one only from the prophecy of Micah. There, reproving the sins of the Jewish rulers, the Lord thus pleads with them by the prophet: "Yet will they lean upon the Lord, and say, Is not the Lord among us? none evil can come upon us. Therefore shall Zion for your sake be plowed as a field, and Jerusalem shall become heaps, and the mountain of the house as the high places of the forest. But in the last days it shall come to pass, that the mountain of the house of the Lord shall be established on the top of the mountains, and be exalted above the hills; and all nations shall flow unto it." (Micah iii. 11, 12; iv. 1.)

The warning in the first part of this passage has been literally accomplished; many now in England have witnessed it with their own eyes. Why should we doubt the literal fulfilment of the rest? Will the Most High God perform His threatenings to the letter, and not fulfil His promises also? Shall the burden of a special curse, because clearly denounced, rest in its full weight upon the unbelieving Jews, and shall not repentant Israel enjoy in all its specialty and fulness the promised blessing? Every suffering, indeed, of the Jews in their long dispersion, is a token of God's righteous anger for their rejection of His own Son. But, blessed be His holy name, it is more. It is a lively pledge that the predictions of coming mercy in their restoration, and conversion, and royal dignity, shall also be visibly accomplished in the sight of men. Indeed that style of interpretation which leaves all the curses in their full weight upon the Jewish nation, and then transfers all the blessings by a figure to the Gentile Church, is no spiritual service to God, but an unrighteous perversion of the truth. The Lord

Himself seems to mark it with the brand of his severe
displeasure, where he declares in connexion with this
very subject, "I hate robbery for burnt offering." (Isa.
lxi. 8.)

The last evidence I shall now adduce, and perhaps
the most impressive of all, is the literal fulfilment of so
many prophecies in the person of our blessed Lord.
None could be more strange and wonderful than these;
none to a merely natural judgment more unlikely to come
to pass. The words of St. Peter, before the events took
place, had a fair show of reason : "Be it far from Thee,'
Lord ; this shall not be unto Thee." (Matt. xvi. 22).
Yet how fully were they all accomplished! The sign
which the Lord gave unto Ahaz was truly "in the height
above, and in the depth beneath," but it was strictly accomplished : "The virgin shall conceive, and shall bear a
son, and they shall call His name Immanuel." (Isa. vii.
10, 11, 14.) The voice of the Baptist was heard in the
wilderness of Judah to "prepare the way of the Lord,
and to make His path straight." (Luke iii. 4.) The Lord,
the messenger of the covenant, came suddenly to His
temple. (Mal. iii. 1.) Glad tidings were preached to the
poor. The eternal Son of God, who " clothes the heavens
with blackness, and makes sackcloth their covering,"
"gave His back to the smiters, and His cheeks to
them that plucked off the hair ; He hid not His face from
shame and spitting." (Isa. l. 3, 5, 6.) The King came
unto Zion, "meek and lowly, sitting on an ass, and a colt
the foal of an ass." (Zech. ix. 9.) "His own familiar
friend, who did eat of His bread," (Ps. xli. 9), laid wait
for Him, and betrayed Him to His enemies. The " Shep-
herd was smitten, and the sheep were scattered abroad."
(Zech. xiii. 7.) They pierced His hands and His feet ;

they gave Him gall to eat; and in his thirst they gave
Him vinegar to drink; they parted His garments among
them, and cast lots upon His vesture. (Ps. lxix. 21;
xxii. 16, 18.) He was brought to the grave with the
wicked, and was with the rich man in His death, and was
numbered with the transgressors. (Isa. liii. 9, 12.) But
the Holy One of God saw no corruption. He rose from
the dead, and the path of life was open before Him into
the presence of His heavenly Father. He ascended on
high, He led captivity captive, and received gifts for men.
(Ps. xvi. 10, 11; lxviii. 18.) And when the work of
atonement was complete, and the heavenly Intercessor
was provided, and the Spirit was poured from on high,
the promise of His Father was at length fulfilled. " I will
also give Thee for a light to the Gentiles, that Thou
mayest be My salvation unto the ends of the earth." (Isa.
lxix. 6.)

But this proof, drawn from the literal accomplishment
of so many prophecies in the person of our Saviour, becomes still more impressive from the manner in which
our Lord Himself, time after time, alludes to that fulfilment. He seeks earnestly to show us that His obedience
was to magnify, not only the law, but also the prophecies
of God. It is in the most solemn scenes of His history
that these passages occur. At the transfiguration " He
answered and told them, how it was written of the Son
of man, that He must suffer many things and be set at
nought." (Mark ix. 12.) At His last approach to Jerusalem He took unto Him the twelve, and said unto them,
" Behold we go up to Jerusalem, and all things that
are written in the prophets concerning the Son of man
shall be accomplished." (Luke xviii. 31.) At the last
supper He repeats the allusion with a solemn addition

—"The Son of man goeth indeed, as it is written of Him, but woe unto that man by whom He is betrayed." (Mark xiv. 21.) On the verge of His bitter agony, the statement is repeated with a fuller emphasis than ever : " For I say unto you, that this which is written must yet be accomplished in me, And He was reckoned among the transgressors ; for even the things which concern Me have their fulfilment." (Luke xxii. 37, comp. Greek text.) This, too, is the cause why in the hour of treachery and darkness He refuses to summon willing legions to His aid— " Thinkest thou that I cannot now pray to my Father, and He shall presently give Me more than twelve legions of angels ? But how then shall the Scriptures be fulfilled, that thus it must be !" (Matt. xxvi. 54.) Nay, even on the cross itself, the Holy Spirit reveals to us the thoughts of the Saviour in His latest agony, and they are still occupied with the same truth : " Jesus knowing that all things were now accomplished, that the Scripture might be fulfilled, saith, I thirst." (John xix. 28.)

What a solemn lesson do these various passages convey ! Sooner than the literal sense of the prophecies should fail, the eternal Son of God stoops cheerfully to shame, to bitter agony, to the death of the cross ! His awful sufferings are endured, not more to accomplish our redemption, than to fulfil in the letter the predictions of God's word, and to maintain unsullied and spotless the veracity of His heavenly Father. Well might St. Paul declare, that " Jesus Christ was a minister of the circumcision *for the truth of God,* to confirm the promises made unto the fathers." (Rom. xv. 8.) And can we, or even dare we, any longer doubt the literal accomplishment, in due season, of all God's prophecies, when it is thus *solemnly assured* to us by the blood of that Divine and glorious sacrifice, which seals to us the covenant of our own salvation?

These arguments for the literal interpretation of prophecy might easily be multiplied and enlarged. But it may be more useful to expose shortly some objections arising from false methods of exposition, which have hindered the reception of its true and simple meaning.

There are two main schools of interpretation, flatly opposed to each other, and which both diverge from the truth, the neological, and the mystical or allegorical. The first is based on the type of the Cerinthian heresy; the second on that of the Gnostic delusion. The first robs the Divine prophecies of their heavenly, the other of their earthly element. The one debases them from their high dignity, to crush them within the passing events of a day; the other unmoors them from all the anchor-hold of time and place, and changes their intense and manifest reality into a vague and mysterious dream. On the first of these it is not needful to dwell, but as the second still prevails in the Church, it may be well to notice some of the objections to which it has given rise.

It has been alleged then, first, on the presumed warrant of some passages in the New Testament, that the title of Jew and the name of Israel belong properly only to true believers in Christ. Thus St. Paul tells us, that "he is not a Jew, which is one outwardly; but he is a Jew, which is one inwardly (Rom. ii. 28); that "all are not Israel, which are of Israel" (Rom. ix. 6); and applies the title of "the Israel of God" to those which walk according to the rule of Christ (Gal. vi. 16).

A close attention to the scope and context of these passages will dissolve the whole objection. The apostle proves, to the unbelieving Jews that their descent from

Abraham, cannot alone avail them for salvation without
faith in Jesus Christ. He admits a hidden and higher
sense in the name of Jew; that he is one who receives
praise from God (Rom. ii. 29), and who offers praise to God
(Gen. xxix. 35). He argues that their natural descent cannot profit them, without this inward character graven on
the heart by God's Holy Spirit. But he nowhere teaches
that the name of Jew, either in history or in prophecy,
is to be commonly taken in this peculiar sense. Nay,
in every case the Holy Spirit seems, in the context, to
guard us expressly against this mistake. Thus, in the
first passage it is added in the very next verse: "What
advantage then hath the Jew ? or what profit is there of
circumcision ? " (Rom. iii. 1), and in the second, after
a few verses : " Israel, which followed after the law of
righteousness, hath not attained to the law of righteousness." (Rom. ix. 31.) And again, when in writing to
the Galatians, he gives the name of Israel to Christian
believers ; it is only after first describing their new creation in Christ Jesus (Gal. iii. 15), and with the emphatic
addition " the Israel of God," to denote those who are in
the actual enjoyment of the Divine favour. But where
there is no special mark of deviation from the usual
sense, the constant use of the terms, Jew, Israel, Zion,
and Jerusalem, in the New Testament writers, instead
of disproving their literal meaning in the Prophets of
the Old Testament, fully ratifies and confirms it.

Again it is alleged, secondly, that since the coming of
Christ all distinction of Jew and Gentile in spiritual
things is at an end, and hence, that no prophecies of
special glory to the Jew can hereafter be literally fulfilled.
So again, St. Paul declares, that " there is no difference
of Jew nor Greek " (Rom. x. 12) ; that " the middle wall

of partition is broken down" (Eph. ii. 14); that in Christ "there is neither Greek nor Jew, circumcision nor uncircumcision, but all are one in Christ Jesus" (Col. ii. 11). And that those who are Christ's are "Abraham's seed, and heirs according to the promise." (Gal. iii. 29.)

These texts, when viewed in their real connexion, are not more conclusive than the former. It is only when read superficially that they seem to clash with the Jewish prophecies. "There is no difference," it is true, "between the Jew and the Greek" in the full and free provision of grace in Jesus Christ, and in the way of attaining salvation by faith in Him—"for the same Lord over all is rich unto all that call upon Him." (Rom. x. 12.) But in the actual measure of faith, in the sovereign dispensation of the gifts of God, in the privilege of visible adoption into the covenant, and the honour which flows from that privilege, there may be, and has been, and is even now, the greatest variety. The Jews, therefore, who, since their rejection, have been the lowest in gospel privileges, and many of them under a sentence of judicial blindness, may yet become, in God's goodness, the highest and the first. "The middle wall of partition" is broken down, which shut out the Gentiles from the temple of God; but yet, within the temple itself, there is an outer and an inner court, and various degrees of privilege and of glory. There is nothing therefore in these passages really inconsistent with a large pre-eminence of Israel in times to come.

The last and most important objection is, the supposed earthly, gross, and carnal character of the literal interpretation. This idea repels many Christians from the subject, and makes them view it as a snare and hindrance rather than a help to the soul. Hence also the title, " spiritual," is often given to the figurative mode of exposition. Let us examine then, by a few plain tests, to which that high title justly belongs.

First, The truly spiritual interpretation is that which calls Faith into the liveliest exercise. For Faith is the nurse and mother of every Christian grace, 'the inlet of all spiritual life to the soul. To which of these two modes of exposition does this character apply ? To that pliant and easy method which receives in the letter whatever accords with our Gentile taste, or chimes in with our favourite system, or falls with a curse on the devoted head of the Jew; and then turns the rest into an allegory to be moulded at our will ? Surely it applies much rather to the literal exposition. For this calls us to the docility of a little child. It bids us cast away our high imaginations, and bring every thought captive to the obedience of Christ, by receiving His messages in their simplest and plainest sense. It commands us, in short, to break down the pride of human systems, and to sacrifice our dearest prejudice, rather than to do violence to one jot or tittle of the Word of God.

Secondly, An interpretation is spiritual, in proportion as it illustrates the harmony and glory of the Divine attributes. In which exposition is this feature most conspicuous ? In the literal, which rests simply on God's veracity, and shows His truth alike displayed in the desolation and the recovery of Israel ;—and not His truth only, but the depths of his long-suffering, and the perseverance of His love, and the triumph of His grace, and the riches of His boundless wisdom ? Or in the figurative, which is based chiefly on the ingenuity of man ; which represents the God of truth as fulfilling His threatenings *in the letter,* but provides an excuse why His promises need not be so fulfilled; and thus destroys the balanced harmony of righteousness and grace, in the providence of the Most High towards the sons of Israel? On the literal view of prophecy, though grievous darkness has rested on the outcast race for two thousand years, the bow of the covenant, bright with hope, is seen still shining over them. On the other view the arch is broken and disappears, and nothing remains of its loveliness but the dark cloud of vengeance.

Again, That interpretation is most spiritual, which magnifies most the truth and preciousness of God's holy word. For this is the grand instrument of our salvation, and God has magnified His word above all His name. But the figurative exposition turns all the prophetic portion into an enigma, which but few can understand, and which must be useless to all others; it first covers the prospect with a deep mist, and then dissuades from further search as unnecessary and even dangerous. While, on the other hand, the literal interpretation leaves it open to our view, just as the Spirit of God has spread it before us, a land of promise, goodly to the eye, with all the rich and varied beauty of earth, and with all the blessed light and purity of heaven.

Lastly, The spiritual interpretation is that which uproots selfishness from the heart, and enthrones on its ruins the love of Christ, and the love of our brethren. But by the figurative interpretation, the Gentile Church is taught to appropriate solely to herself all the promises of God, where Israel, Judah, and Jerusalem are most clearly addressed; regardless of the wrong done to the outcasts of Zion, and of the dark cloud which is thus brought over that glorious attribute of her Lord, His truth and faithfulness. On the other hand, the literal interpretation leads us to rejoice, with a pure and unselfish joy, in the fulness of God's love to His ancient people. It calls us, as Gentile Christians, to be willing ourselves to decrease, if only the faithfulness of our Lord may be vindicated and His glory increased; and our own heart's desire and prayer be fulfilled in the salvation of Israel.

I have thus shown the full warrant which God has given to His Church for the literal interpretation of prophecy, from His own express command, from the nature of the prophecies themselves, from the conduct of the apostles, the history of the Jewish nation, and from the solemn and repeated declarations of the Lord Jesus. I have shown its consistency with the statements of the Apostle of the Gentiles, and its peculiar claim, above every other, to the title of a spiritual interpretation.

CHAPTER IV.

FROM age to age some few, or even many have been
the prey of a dangerous excitement, followed by a re-
lapse no less dangerous, when the season of false hope
was gone by.   But the great body, except in one or two
grand epidemics of alarm, have been at all times in a
deep sleep, like the sleep of death.   The temptations on
either side have been gaining in strength.   The fact that
we are now 1800 years nearer the Advent, than when
St. Paul wrote, must in times of alarm render the fever
more intense, and the excitement more dangerous, than
with the Thessalonians.   On the other hand, the fact
that sixty generations have passed since such warnings
were first given, supplies a pretext for indifference, which
grows more plausible in each successive age than in the
previous one, to those Christians who are lying down and
loving to slumber.   No remedy can be found for these
opposite evils, but a growing knowledge of those times
which God has revealed for our guidance.   A view of the
calm and stedfast course of Providence in past ages, and
its fulfilled intervals of patient delay, will free us from the
snare of the Thessalonian Church.   We shall not then
suffer uncertain conjectures, centred on some one moment
of time, to exert that influence which is due only to the
broad and solemn reality of eternal judgment.   But the
same insight into the past course of God's Providence

will reveal to us clearly, the sure approach of the great day of the Lord. We shall no longer fancy it, as worldly men do in their secret thoughts, to be a rainbow dream, that flies away from us as we advance in the stream of time. We shall see it as the storm-tost mariner sees the distant headlands ; a land of promise, whose place is fixed in the charts of heaven, though our eyes may sometimes deceive us as to its distance. And we shall feel certain that every day is bringing us nearer to the glorious haven, and is hastening us to the close of the mystery of God. And now that the voyage of the Church has lasted so long, the dimness is beginning to clear from the horizon, and we may see plainly that we are rapidly nearing the shore; that we are living in the last days, and the glory of the Lord will soon be revealed. Every day therefore it becomes more needful for the Church to discern the times and seasons, if she would escape the threatening dangers on the right hand and on the left, and be prepared as a chaste virgin for the coming of her Lord.

But here the question may arise, However useful such knowledge might be, is it not entirely beyond our reach ? Has not the Father reserved the times in His own power? Is not the history of all such researches a catalogue.of rash and groundless conjectures, soon refuted by time ?

To answer this doubt let us consult the record of past ages in the Word of God. Here we learn that such knowledge has been revealed, though sparingly, from the earliest ages, and has served for the practical guidance of the people of God.

In the old world the light of divine truth shone very dimly. The hope of redemption was only like moonlight in the thick darkness. Yet even then, this knowledge *was not* wholly denied. Enoch, the seventh from Adam, prophesied, with holy solemnity, the coming of the Lord, to the scoffers of his own generation. And as the flood, an awful type of the last judgment, drew nearer, Noah had the season of forbearance plainly revealed. " My · Spirit shall not always strive with man for that he also is flesh ; yet his days shall be an hundred and twenty years." No announcement of time could be more clear and simple. Warned by this voice of God and its attendant threatenings, Noah " moved with fear, prepared an ark for the saving of his house." He thus learned to possess his soul in patience amidst the scorning of the proud, till the last sands of this hour-glass of heaven were run out, and the flood came on the world of the ungodly.

The next main era of trial was the captivity of Egypt. Here the time was doubly revealed in years and generations. " Know of a surety," the Lord said to Abraham, " that thy seed shall be a stranger in a land that is not theirs, and shall serve them ; and they shall afflict them four hundred years " (Gen. xv. 13). This message of God was forgotten by the great body of the people, whose eyes went after the idols of Egypt. But in the heart of Moses it was deeply treasured, and made him willing to suffer with the people of God, and eager to effect their deliverance. He was himself in the fourth generation from the patriarch Levi, and knew that nearly four centuries had passed from the call and sojourning of Abraham, at the time when he slew the Egyptian and sought to deliver his brethren. True, even Moses, like many Christians, antedated the time of mercy, and forty years were to be spent in lonely exile before the season of redemption was come. But still his faith in that promise to Abraham had a blessed reward. That same " Moses whom they

refused, saying, Who made thee a ruler and a judge ? the
same did God send to be a ruler and a deliverer by the
hand of the angel which appeared to him in the bush "
(Acts vii. 35). They who despised the prediction of the
times and seasons were left unprepared, and perished in
the wilderness. He who laid it up in his heart, and erred
only in the eagerness of his hope and desire, was tried
with a season of delay; but he obtained the fulness of the
blessing, and became the ruler and deliverer of the people
of God.

The sojourn in the wilderness was the next period of
temptation. Once more the time was plainly foretold,
that the faith of the servants of God might not sink
under the delay. " Ye shall wander," it was said, " in
the wilderness forty years " (Num. xiv. 33). It might still
be doubtful whether the period began from the Exodus
itself, or from the date of the threatening. But still, in
the fortieth year, when Aaron died, no one who believed
that message could doubt that the deliverance was close
at hand; and their faith and courage would thus be
strengthened for the warfare. " All these things," as
St. Paul tells us, " happened unto them as types;" for
the Christian Church was also to abide long in the wilderness; " and they are written for our admonition on whom
the latter times of the world are come " (1 Cor. x. 11).

While open miracles were wrought under the judges,
and during the glory of David and Solomon, no distinct
times were revealed; but when the kingdoms of Israel
and Judah were sinking into ruin, this Divine light was
vouchsafed again to the Church. When Ahaz was in the
deep estalarm, and the heart of his people was " moved as
the trees of the wood are moved by the wind," a prophecy
of numbered years was given once more to quiet the

fears of God's people. Judgment on Israel and mercy to Judah were proclaimed in the same message: "Within threescore and five years shall Ephraim be broken, that it be no more a people" (Isa. viii. 2, 8). After a pause of seven centuries, this prediction of times was made the preface to that glorious prophecy which announced the birth of Immanuel, and the wonderful mystery of our Saviour's birth, the Son of the Virgin, God manifest in the flesh.

The captivity of Judah soon followed. This time of sorrow had also its bounds assigned in a twice-repeated prophecy. "This whole land shall be a desolation and an astonishment; and these nations shall serve the king of Babylon seventy years" (Jer. xxv. 11.) And again, "After seventy years are accomplished at Babylon, I will visit you, and perform My good word to you, in causing you to return to this place" (Jer. xxix. 10). The precise date might be obscure till the period was near its close, for there were three events from which it might begin, and two of them were actually marked, after seventy years, by a signal deliverance. But still the time itself of the exiles was clear, and the promise well-suited to sustain the faith in those years of sorrow.

The prophecy also was not given to be buried in neglect until after its fulfilment. The holy Daniel, the wisest of men, knew better its gracious design. Two years before its earlier close he "understood by reckoning the number of the years, whereof the word of the Lord came to Jeremiah the prophet, that he would accomplish seventy years in the desolations of Jerusalem" (Dan. ix. 2). His search into this unfulfilled prediction of times and seasons first gave light to his mind, and then stirred him up to deep confession and earnest prayer. Man might denounce it as presumption, or despise it as folly; but God rewarded it by the vision of an angel and the gift of a new prophecy, which has been one main bulwark of the Christian faith in every succeeding age.

In the vision of Gabriel, and the prophecy of the seventy weeks, the series of revealed times is continued to the First Advent of our Lord. Whatever doubts might rest on their exact termination, they served to guide and animate the hopes of the Jewish believers. Simeon and Anna, when our Lord was born, were resting on this prophecy, and waiting for the consolation of Israel. As the faith of Daniel in the words of Jeremiah, so too that of holy Simeon in the prediction of Daniel, was rewarded with further light; and "it was revealed to him that he should not see death until he had seen the Lord's Messiah." And thus his faith in times still unfulfilled awoke that song of praise which the Church repeats evermore in her solemn worship, down to the present day. If we despise or denounce a humble search into the dates of prophecy, our own lips bear witness against us, every time that we borrow those words of deep and holy thanksgiving.

Finally, the words of our Lord which announced the fall and ruin of the temple within one generation, were the safety of the early disciples in the hour of danger, and ensured their deliverance when Jerusalem was overthrown. And thus, from first to last, definite intervals have been revealed to the Church, whether for grace or judgment; and a prayerful humble search into their meaning, before their fulfilment, has ever brought with it increase of light and the assurance of a blessing.

But here doubts and difficulties have arisen, and have led many Christians to neglect the lesson which these various examples lend for our guidance. Let us examine the most usual and most important of these, and we shall find them to be shadowy and vain; and that the duty of seeking insight into the seasons God has revealed, will only stand out in fuller and brighter relief.

First, we are often reminded that "secret things belong unto the Lord our God" (Deut. xxix. 29). And, doubtless, even in searching God's holy prophecies, the spirit of that caution may be transgressed by a vain curiosity and irreverent boldness. But when the words are perverted into an absolute prohibition, the rest of the verse supplies a conclusive answer. "The things that are revealed belong to us and our children." Surely every part of God's word is a revelation. To number it among the secret things which are best honoured by neglect, is really to fling back the Divine gift in the face of Him who bestows it. He declares solemnly that all inspired Scripture is profitable for us, and that whatever is written therein is written for our learning. Who are we, that we should pretend to be wiser than God, or profess that some of His revealed sayings would have been more wisely kept back from us? as if our neglect were to remedy the unwise loquacity of the Spirit of God.

The words of our Lord to His apostles have given rise to another scruple: "It is not for you to know the times or the seasons which the Father hath put in His own power" (Acts i. 7). These, however, when searched narrowly, are a strong warrant for an inquiry into the times and seasons of prophecy, while they suggest a needful caution for its due exercise. The words are not general, as our version seems to imply, but special. "It is not for you to know *the* times and seasons which the Father hath reserved in His own power." There is here a direct allusion to a text familiar to the apostles, and which explains the true meaning of the answer. Daniel (chapter xii.) had heard two angels put the inquiry, "How long shall it be to the end of these wonders?" The Son of God replies with a solemn oath, that "It shall be for a season and seasons and half a season, and when he shall have accomplished to scatter the power of the holy people, all these things shall be finished." The prophet then asks for further light, but receives the answer, "The words are closed up and sealed till the time of the end."

The answer, then, of our Lord to His apostles on earth is only the echo of His reply to the prophet in the vision. The event spoken of is clearly the same in both, the restoration of the kingdom to Israel, and the end of the scattering of the holy people. The seasons of delay before that event were sealed till the time of the end; until then the Father, by the lips of the covenant angel, had expressly reserved them in His own power. The disciples asked the *time* of that restoration. Our Lord, as if pointing them to the words of Daniel, introduces the very term employed in the vision, "It is not for you to know the times *or the seasons* which the Father hath put in His own power." As if He had said, The time of which you speak follows certain seasons of predicted delay; and these seasons have been reserved at present from a complete revelation, until the Father Himself, at the time of the end, shall begin to unseal them.

We have thus a threefold and fourfold answer to the objection. First, the words are not general as to all times, but refer specially to the three times and a half which were to be sealed and closed until a later period. Secondly, they are not general as to Christians, but relate, with a marked emphasis, to the apostles themselves, and Christians in their day. "Such knowledge," our Lord *implies*, "may be hereafter given to others, but it is not

for you. Another work is assigned you, to found the
Church and spread the gospel through the world. It is
only when the faith of the Gentiles begins to decay that
the Father will unseal the times of that blessed hope,
which will be as life from the dead to the unbelieving
world. And hence, further, they are a secret assurance
that there will be other Christians of a later age to whom
these times will be unsealed, as those of Jeremiah were
to Daniel himself, shortly before their close. Finally,
there were other times not reserved which the apostles
themselves might know, as the fall of Jerusalem and of
the Temple in their own generation.

But this leads us to the words of Christ in the prophecy on the mount, which are often viewed as a clear
censure on all these inquiries: "Of that day and that
hour knoweth no man, no, not the angels which are in
heaven, neither the Son, but the Father" (Mark xiii. 32).
How far the spirit of this caution extends may require
much spiritual wisdom to determine; but conclusions
loosely and rashly drawn from it have nothing to sustain
them. First, the assertion is strictly true only of the time
when our Saviour spoke; for, surely, with regard to the
Son of God, they must have ceased to be true when He was
risen and ascended into glory. Our Lord Himself, since
they were uttered, has received in His human nature im-
measurable wisdom; and we may infer that His Church
also, though in measures infinitely short of His own, will
receive from age to age a like increase. Again, the
words refer to the day and hour, but not to the year,
much less to the generation in which that great event will
occur. Minute conjectures on the time of the Advent may
still be forbidden us, and the spirit of the caution may
extend itself beyond the strict letter. But still the spirit

of the previous verse has a voice not less plain, and speaks with the same authority. The first generation of the Church there is made a precedent for the last; and leads us to expect that Christians, whenever that generation has come, will be able to ascertain it, and may know by clear signs that the Lord is really near at hand.

Again, it is alleged by some Christians that no materials really exist for that search into the times which so many examples appear to warrant. They suppose that the Church has been left more than two thousand years without any such period being revealed which might mark out the distance or nearness of the end. Surely it would be strange if a light, vouchsafed to the Church from the first building of the ark to the fall of Jerusalem and the flight to Pella, had suddenly ceased under the nobler and clearer dispensation of the Gospel. And when all resort to observers of times is strictly forbidden, because the Prophet like unto Moses was to appear, it would be still more marvellous if the coming of that great Prophet were to be the very signal for the withholding all knowledge of times from the Church of God. But, in fact, while only about seven distinct periods were revealed in prophecy from the creation to the birth of our Lord, there are at least twice the number which clearly relate to times after the First Advent. The Church of the New Testament, therefore, instead of being condemned to total darkness, has been favoured with a double portion of light and more abundant revelations; though, for the fuller exercise of her faith and wisdom, the seasons have now been set before her in a more mysterious form, and greater care is needful to decipher their true meaning.

One last prejudice remains, the most suited for popular *use; and yet,* when viewed practically, the most deceptive. All inquiry into prophetic times, it is often said, is fruitless and unprofitable. Failure after failure has occurred in the most confident anticipations, till the melancholy series of errors and disappointments should warn us from entering on so barren a field.

This caution and censure, within certain limits is just, beyond those limits it is presumptuous and wrong. When we venture to fix the month or the day of coming events; or confidently assign even the exact year, especially of that Advent which was once hidden from the Son of Man, and is still wrapped in a mysterious veil; we slight the lessons of experience, and run counter to the spirit and scope of the words of Christ on Mount Olivet. On the other hand, to ascertain our true place in the decrees of Providence, and the prophetic features of the generation in which we live; nay, even conjectures, offered with caution and humility, on the year when revealed numbers may expire, are justified by the examples of Scripture, and encouraged and commended by the Spirit of God. If Daniel had been guilty of sin when he reckoned up the years from Jeremiah's prediction, and found that only two remained, he would never have been recompensed for a presumptuous error by the visit of Gabriel, and the revelation of another prophecy still more glorious.

To condemn the inquiry, within these limits, is really to annul the command of Christ, "Search the Scriptures," and contradicts the plain voice of the Spirit of God. The prophets themselves, we are told, inquired and searched diligently what time, or "what manner of time, the Spirit of Christ which was in them did signify." The blessed angels no less "desire to look into" these things, and are seen in successive visions applying for light and knowledge to the Son of God. With such examples, of saints upon earth and angels in heaven, we may well scorn the ridicule of the scorner, and disregard vain censures of ignorant or faithless Christians.

For, in truth, these inquiries, when pursued in humility, have never been really fruitless. Their true object is, not to construct for us beforehand an exact chronology of coming ages; though not a few modest conjectures on the very year of coming events, drawn from the prophecies, have been strikingly fulfilled. But such a test of their worth is miserably false and deceptive. The great use of these revealed times is to shield Christians from two opposite evils,—a blind and impatient hope, such as would fever and disturb the soul, and a deadly and fatal slumber, which removes the coming of the Lord into the far distance, and folds the hands in contented worldliness. Whenever these times have been searched into with humility and prayer, both dangers have been averted. The exact season of the end, it is true, may have been often antedated, and distant events foreshortened in the prospect; but still the practical benefits were secured. The faithful have neither been " shaken in mind nor troubled" by a feverish and impatient hope, that overlooks the calm progress of God's counsels; nor yet have been suffered to say in their hearts, with the evil servant, " My Lord delayeth His coming." By these prophetic seasons, and by these only, the balance has been restored between opposite graces, the patient waiting for Christ, and earnest and assured hope in the approach of His blessed kingdom.

Let us now inquire the degrees and measures in which *this knowledge* of the times is bestowed, and may reason-

ably be expected by the Church. And here there are a
few general maxims, which seem to be clearly set before
us in the Word of God.

First, the knowledge of which we now speak must
remain ever hidden from the unbelieving and ungodly.
"None of the wicked shall understand" (Dan. xii. 10).
In their case, even to the last, the vision of all the prophets
remains "as the words of a book that is sealed." These
deeper things of God are set forth in such a manner, that
only by a patient and believing search can we attain their
real meaning.

Unbelieving and curious men may doubtless receive
on trust the conclusions of others; but only as a fashion-
able creed which, at the first change of the fashion, is
cast aside. These times are revealed in connection with
the deepest views of God's Providence, with solemn
warnings of judgment, and mysteries of human sin and
Divine forbearance, which only spiritual minds can understand. Hence the Holy Spirit warns us, that worldly
men, even to the last, will walk in darkness; and in the
time when they are saying, "Peace and safety," the
times of delay will be gone, and sudden destruction over-
take them as a thief in the night (1 Thes. v. 3).

Again, such knowledge can only be gained, even by
true Christians, when sought with humble prayer and
devout reverence. It was in answer to such prayers that
most of these times were announced at first; and only
such petitions as obtained the messages themselves, can
remove the Divine seal which has rested on them for
ages. The two last visions of Daniel, in which these
numbers chiefly occur, were each given in the hour of
his deepest confession; and the numbers in the Apocalypse, as well as the visions that contain them, were given

to the beloved John after reverent prostration at the
footstool of Christ and weeping. It is the meek, and the
meek only, whom God will guide in judgment, and to
whom He will teach His way. When even pious Christians, learned or unlearned, begin to quarrel with God's
prophecies instead of searching them with reverence,
their learning will become folly, their strength like
Samson's will pass from them, and they will be left like
the unbeliever to stumble on in darkness.

The measure of light vouchsafed to the Church, and
attainable by each Christian, increases from age to age.
Under the Old Testament, one period after another was
revealed ; and the true limits of each in its turn became
clear as its end was approaching. It was near the close
of the Egyptian captivity that Moses began to discern
the time ; and near the end of the captivity at Babylon
that Daniel understood by reckonings the number of
the years. It was when the predicted weeks had almost
run out that Simeon was waiting for Messiah, and had
the promise given that he should see the Lord's Christ.
The same principle is true also under the Gospel.
Prophetic times have been revealed from the first ; but
the Divine seal, placed on many of them, was to be
slowly removed. Every century as it rolled on, lessened
the motives for concealment, and increased the need for
a partial unveiling of the times, to sustain and guide the
hopes of the Church. The declarations that the end was
near would afterwards have become a snare to the faith
of Christians, as they have been to infidels, unless it were
shown that the delay also was predicted, and a limit
assigned for its continuance in the word of God itself.
And surely if, in those first ages, the ignorance of the
Church was a strong motive for watchfulness, so when the

end is really near and within one generation, an assured
knowledge of its nearness will be a motive still more
powerful, and one which the Lord will not withhold from
His faithful people.

This promise, indeed, of growing light, is repeatedly
given, and in various forms. It is in the time of the end
that many are to run to and fro, and knowledge of the
word of prophecy is to be increased. " In the eventide "
of the Gospel dispensation "there will be light " (Zech.
xiv. 7). Although the " wicked " remain in darkness to
the last, " the wise shall understand." When the Eastern
Empire of Rome has fallen under the scourge of the
second woe, and the light of the Reformation dawns on
the visible Church of the West and its demon worshippers, the open book of prophecy is to be read once more,
and digested more deeply by the faithful (Rev. ix. x. 8, 9).
Finally, in the times of the last vial the cloud is to be
rolled away from the temple of God, and the ark of His
covenant, rich with all the messages of His holy prophets,
is to be seen openly unveiled (Rev. xv. 5, 8 ; xvi. 17).
There are thus distinct and successive stages in this
increase of light, in the first opening of the Gospel and
the time of St. John, in the latter times of apostasy,
in the dawn of the Reformation, and in that outpouring
of the last vial, which seems to be now close at hand.

Further, this promise of growing light not only belongs to different ages of the Church, but in the same
age to every individual Christian, as he advances in holiness and searches more deeply into the word of God. He
will thus obtain a fuller knowledge of these truths, or a
deeper and firmer grasp on the truths already made
known to him. Where the religion of the heart is neglected, no curious search into times can hope for a Divine

blessing. And even where there is growth in holiness, this special gift can only be looked for when there are special desires and prayers for its attainment, and the means of knowledge are wisely improved. But where there is both a general and special preparation, this precious gift of the Spirit will be vouchsafed in larger and larger measure. Daniel was marked from his early years by eminent grace; yet it was not until he and his companions had desired mercy of the God of heaven for this secret, that even the first vision was revealed to him. In each later prophecy earnest prayer and confession led the way, or earnest inquiry followed the Divine message. The God of Daniel is the same yesterday, to-day, and for ever. When we search His word with prayer and reverence, He will still reveal to us its hidden wonders, and all that is safe or profitable for His children to know. We shall gain such knowledge of the times, clearer and clearer to the last, as may quicken our zeal and guide our hopes, and prepare us for the coming of the Lord; and the rest will be wisely and graciously reserved from us, as from the beloved prophet; until we also stand in our lot in the end of the days, when these times and seasons shall lose themselves in a sea of glory in the kingdom of God.

May we, like the men of Issachar, " have understanding of the times, to know what the servants of God ought to do " (1 Chron. xii. 32). Let us not continue in the sleep of worldliness and in the darkness of sin. Let our knowledge of the times lead us to prepare for eternity. Let us, amidst the signs of approaching judgment, shelter our souls in the covenant of grace; and cast away the works of darkness and clothe ourselves with the armour of light; because we see the day approaching, and the morning of the resurrection may be near at hand. Let us take to ourselves the " breastplate of faith and love, and for an helmet the hope of salvation," so, whatever changes may be at hand, our souls will be sheltered in the chambers of Divine mercy, and the short night of fear and trouble be speedily followed by the blessed morning of everlasting joy, " the Sabbath-keeping that remaineth for the people of God."

CHAPTER V.

HAVING now shown from Scripture, that progressive knowledge and further in sight into the prophetic times is promised in the last days to reverent and patient study, I proceed in a closing chapter briefly to unfold those further thoughts on the times and seasons of sacred prophecy, which have resulted from the continued meditation of later years on the prophetic Scriptures, and on the course of God's Providence.

I. *The History of the World a Week of Millennia.*

The whole history of the world has been held for the last two thousand years, by a very general consent, to be in the Divine plan a week of Millennia. This was obscurely revealed from the first, as is implied in Gen. i. when compared with 2 Pet. iii. 8 and Ps. xc. 4. The same view was current among the Jews before Christ, under the name of the tradition of the house of Elias.

The following are some of the successive testimonies from early times to this simple and grand conception.

1. EPISTLE OF BARNABAS (c. 15), A.D. 70.

"God in six days created the work of His hands, and in the seventh day He rested and sanctified it. What does it mean that He completed it in six days? It means that the Lord will accomplish all things in six thousand years. For a day with Him is a thousand years, and He Himself bears witness, saying, 'A day shall be as a thousand years.' Therefore, my children, in six days, in six thousand years, all things shall be perfected. ' And He rested on the seventh.' This means that when His Son shall come, He will end the time of the Lawless One, and will judge the unholy, and will change the sun and the moon and the stars, so that then He will rest gloriously on the seventh day."

2. THE PSEUDO-ENOCH, A.D. 150–200 arranges the history of the world in ten weeks, of which every day is a century.

3. IRENÆUS, adv. Haer. v. *ad fin.*, A.D. 150.

" In as many days as the world was made, in so many a thousand fold it will be completed. The Scripture says, ' The heaven and the earth were finished and all the host of them; and God ended in the sixth day His works which He made, and God rested in the seventh day from all the works of His hands.' This is a narrative of the things that have come to pass, and a prophecy of those that will be; for a day of the Lord is a thousand years."

4. CYPRIAN, De Exh. Mart. c. 11, A.D. 250.

" First in the Divine arrangement were seven days, containing seven thousands of years."

5. LACTANTIUS, Inst. vii. 14, A.D. 300.

" As in six days all the works of God were completed, it is needful that the world should continue in this state through the ages of six thousand years; and again, as He rested on the seventh day and blessed it, it is needful that in the close of the six thousand years, all wickedness should be abolished from the earth, and that justice should reign through a thousand years."

6. VICTORINUS, On Creation, A.D. 300.

" To those seven days, the Lord attributed to each 1000 years, for thus went the warning, In thine eyes O Lord a thousand years are as one day. Therefore the

true Sabbath will be in the 7th millenary of years, and
then Christ and His elect shall reign."

7. AMBROSE, in Luc. viii. 23, A.D. 400.

"Because in the seventh day God rested from all His
works, after a week of that created world eternal rest is
promised."

8. AUGUSTINE, Ep. 199. "The End of the Age," A.D. 400.

"'It is the last hour' (1 John ii. 18), which some thus
understand, that six thousand years constitute as it were
one day, and they divide that into twelve parts, as it were
hours, so that the last 500 years would seem to be the
last hour, of which they affirm John was speaking when
he said that it was 'the last hour.'"

9. THE CHRONICLE OF EUSEBIUS, A.D. 400.

Makes the six thousand years to end A.D. 800.

10. SULPITIUS SEVERUS, A.D. 550.

Makes A.D. 400 to be A.M. 5819, so making A.D. 581 to
be the end of six thousand years.

Several of these references are here borrowed from
Mr. Elliott, *Horæ Apocalypticæ,* iv. 701, 702 (5th ed.)

The series might easily be continued if time allowed, by
many writers of the intervening centuries, and is fitly
closed by the beautiful utterance of our Christian poet
Cowper, towards the close of the last century.

"The groans of Nature in this nether world,
  Which Heaven has heard for ages, have an end,
  Foretold by prophets and by poets sung,
  Whose fire was kindled at the prophets' lamp,
  The time of rest, the promised Sabbath comes,
  Six thousand years of sorrow have well nigh
  Fulfilled their tardy and disastrous course
  Over a sinful world; and what remains
  Of this tempestuous state of human things,

Is merely as the working of a sea
Before a calm, that rocks itself to rest :
For He, whose car the winds are, and the clouds
The dust that waits upon his sultry march,
When sin hath moved him and his wrath is hot,
Shall visit earth in mercy ; shall descend
Propitious in his chariot paved with love ;
And what his storms have blasted and defaced
For man's revolt, shall with a smile repair."
Winter Walk at Noon.

II. *The Septuagint Chronology.*

The genealogies in Genesis differ in the Hebrew text, the Samaritan Pentateuch, and the Septuagint version. The chronology in this last, received generally by the Eastern Church from the beginning of the Christian era until now, places the creation of the world about B.C. 5500. This Septuagint addition of 1500 years to the genealogies in Genesis, fulfilled to the early Church a practical purpose, foreshortening the interval of delay till the return of Christ, reducing it from 2000 to 500 years, or to one-fourth of the real interval, since the completion of 6000 years would thus correspond to A.D. 500, instead of A.D. 2000.

The general opinion of the Jews was, that the world was to be 2000 years without the Law, 2000 years under the Law, and 2000 years under Messiah ; this is still called by them a tradition of Elias, an eminent rabbi who lived before the birth of Christ ; who also taught that in the seventh millennary the earth would be renewed, and the righteous dead raised, no more to turn again to dust ; that the just then alive should mount up with wings as eagles, and in that day they need not fear though the mountains should be cast into the midst of the sea.

(Elliott "Horæ Apocalypticæ," iv. p. 701, quoting Mede.)

The most current chronology in modern times is that of Archbishop Ussher, based on the Hebrew numbers. His date for the Creation, Gen. i., is B.C. 4004, and the true date of the Nativity is B.C. 4. This makes an interval of four exact millennia from the Creation to the Nativity.

Mr. Clinton, the best of recent chronologers, like Ussher and Augustine, argues strongly for the genuineness of the Hebrew numbers, in contrast to the Septuagint or the Samaritan Pentateuch. But Clinton differs from Ussher by taking the period of the Judges as 134 years longer, so as to place the date of the Creation B.C. 4138. Thus, in Clinton's reckoning, the destruction of the temple by Titus, A.D. 70, would be 4208 A.M. Now, this latest chronology is both confirmed and anticipated by the Pseudo-Enoch, whose own real date is not B.C. 150 (as placed by Dr. Westcott, following Ewald), but more than three centuries later, from A.D. 150–200; this may be proved by many arguments. He divides the 7000 years of the world into ten weeks of 700 years, each day being a century. Thus his seventh week would be A.M. 4200–4900; and the first event in his summary of that week is the destruction of the "House of Glory." This accords exactly with the chronology of Clinton, with whom A.D. 70 is 4208.

III. *The Chronology of Modern Geologists.*

Modern geological speculators would replace the chronology of Scripture by a tissue of conjectures of " science falsely so called," groping in the dark amidst the *débris* and drift of the deluge, and pretending to frame a chronology for which definite data are wholly wanting. Geology can discover, and has discovered many facts with regard to the past changes of the earth; but a chronology of the duration of consecutive periods of terrestrial

change prior to the genesis of man and the commence
ment of human testimony, is just the one thing plainly
out of its reach, in the absence of many needful data, the
lack of which geologists usually ignore. The chronology
of geologists has its birth in a "land of darkness, as
darkness itself, of the shadow of death, without any order,
where the light is as darkness" (Job x. 21, 22). The
only scientific ground for a widely different theory, which
would place the creation of man 500,000 years distant, is
that of Mr. Croll, which I have fully disproved in a paper
read before the Victoria Institute in 1878. (See "Journal
of Transactions," 1879–80 ; also " Scripture Doctrine of
Creation.")

The true chronology of Scripture has its starting-point
in that sublime message, " The Spirit of God moved upon
the face of the waters. And God said, Let there be light :
and there was light. And God saw the light, that it was
good : and God divided the light from the darkness."
Thus the whole revealed history of the world, the land of
light and order, is parted off by that first day of creation
from indefinite ages of night and chaos which had gone
before, and reaches on through 7000 years of the world's
history to the new heavens and new earth ; " the race of
time, till time stand fixed."

> " New heavens, new earth, ages of endless date
> Founded in righteousness and peace and love,
> To bring forth fruits, joy and eternal bliss."

IV. The next question is the more exact definition of
the millennial unit, that is, the exact length of each of
the seven millennia. For a millennium may not be pre-
cisely a thousand years. A period of 1005, or 335×3
years, or a period of 1008, or 168×6 years would be a
millennium.

There are several intervals between ten and eleven centuries, for which there is some presumption.

(1) One thousand years exact, as in Ussher's chronology.

(2) One thousand and twenty years, which is 34 prophetic months, instead of 33⅓.

(3) One thousand and forty years, which is the most complete and exact soli-lunar cycle.

(4) One thousand and fifty years, or 35 complete prophetic months, and fifteen terms of human life of seventy years. Ps. xc. 10.

(5) One thousand and eighty years, which is three prophetic times, or 36 prophetic months.

As in the common reckonings of time there are several days of slightly different length, sidereal and solar, and in like manner several months, varying from 27½ to 30½ days; and several years, from the lunar year of twelve lunations, or 354 days, to the Egyptian year of 360 days, the Julian of 365 days, and the Julian intercalated, 365¼ days; it is reasonable to suppose something analogous in the reckoning of the great millennial period. Taking the chronology of Clinton, which I believe to be the best, we have first 2083 years, from the Creation to the birth of Isaac, the great type of the Messiah in whom all the nations of the earth were to be blessed. From the birth of Isaac we have 2055 years to the Nativity, or 2085 years to the Resurrection and Ascension of the true Isaac into heaven. 2000 years more would bring us to the year of the world 6168, or of the Christian era 2030.

The seventh millennial period, or the "millennium," is followed by a "little season," of which the length is not defined, of the loosing of Satan (Rev. xx. 3). The 168 years of surplus of the first six millennia are just one-sixth of a millennium, or four hours of a great millennial day. If the "little season" after the millennium were of the same length, this would be a total excess of one-third of a millennium in the whole 7000 years. This is 335 years, the very same excess over a thousand which we find in the last number of Daniel, of 335 prophetic days, followed by the promise to the prophet, "Thou shalt rest, and stand in thy lot at the end of the days."

As it seems one part of the Divine plan so to reveal the times, that the hope of the Church should always be elastic to the extent of one prophetic month of 30 years, or half a generation, it is plainly possible that of these five prophetic months, one might precede instead of following the millennium, in which case its commencement, instead of A.D. 2030, would only arrive in A.D. 2060. There are three different units, subordinate to the great interval of a millennium, which reveal themselves in the sacred calendar of prophecy. The first is the prophetic month of 30 years, analogous in the year-day scale to the natural month of 30 days, and itself a soli-lunar cycle. The second is 33⅓ years, or one-third of a century, or one-thirtieth of a millennium. This is the length of our Lord's earthly life. It may be called the soli-lunar unit, being that which harmonizes the two great calendars, the Christian and the Mahometan; for 33⅓ solar years equal 34⅓ lunar years. A third unit is 42 years, which is one HOUR, or one twenty-fourth of the millennial day; this again is to the last unit in the proportion of 5 to 4. The interval just mentioned as the surplus of the six thousand years, is five soli-lunar units, or four millennial hours. A like epact or supplement of the millennium would make a total of ten soli-lunar units, or eight millennial hours. The total duration of the world on this view would be 6000 years increased by 1335, the last number in Daniel.

The commencement of the millennium on this view would probably be A.D. 2030, plus or minus 30; that is, from A.D. 2000 to A.D. 2060; the minus sign would answer to the hypothesis of a shortening of the days, mentioned as possible (Matt. xxiv. 22); and the plus sign would answer to the transfer of thirty years to the opening of the millennium from the close. This latitude of two generations in the revelation of the "times" tends to keep that revelation from becoming the food of a blind fatalism. Thus the fixity of the Divine plan is kept from crushing out the sense of man's responsibility, and full scope is given for the notable promise, (Jer. xviii. 7-9): "At what instant I shall speak concerning a nation, and concerning a kingdom, to pluck up, and to pull down, and to destroy it; if that nation, against whom I have pronounced, turn from their evil, I will repent of the evil that I thought to do unto them. . . . Speak to the men of Judah, and to the inhabitants of Jerusalem, saying, Thus saith the Lord; Behold, I frame evil against you, and devise a device against you: return ye now every one from his evil way, and make your ways and your doings good." So we are taught in the message to Nineveh (Jon. iii. 9, 10): "Who can tell if God will turn and repent, and turn away from His fierce anger, that we perish not? . . . And God repented of the evil, that He had said that He would do unto them; and He did it not." Thus the destruction of Nineveh was deferred for an interval not expressly revealed.

How certainly it came at last, we have an emphatic proof in all the Nineveh remains which are now stored in the British Museum, and accessible to every eye.

V. *The number of the Beast and its prophetical significance.*

Besides the χρόνος and the oath of the covenant angel
(chap. x. 5–7), the Apocalypse contains two other main
data of a prophetic chronology—the number of the beast,
chap. xiii. 18, and the series of the seven or eight heads
of the beast, as defined chap. xvii. 9–14. These three
strands of the Divine cable are closely intertwined, and
gain increased strength from their union.

The number of the beast combines at least three
characters :—a definition of the name, an indication of
the date or chronology, and a further indication of its
moral features.

First, the name is Lateinos, as early taught by Irenæus,
but also ἡ Λατινὴ βασιλεία. Mr. Clarke drew up a list of
almost a thousand names of kingdoms, ancient or modern,
and found that none of these except ἡ Λατινὴ βασιλεία,
when the values of its Greek letters are summed up, gives
the total of 666. Thus the beast is the Latin kingdom,
the fourth or Roman empire in the Latin stage of its
development.

But the number is also a date of the commencement of
the power of the beast, as implied by its contrast to the
42 months in the same prophecy. It occupies the same
place in the Revelation as the final date in Daniel of 1335
days. Now the sum of these two is 2001. The main outline of the world's history is three bi-millennial periods,
followed by the millennium, or Sabbath of rest. The third
of these periods is made up of the number of the beast,
and the 1335 days of which it is said to the prophet Daniel,
"Thou shalt rest, and stand in thy lot at the end of the
days." The whole period is thus trisected into three equal
parts. The close of the first third, A.D. 663, is marked

by the nativity of the beast, and since B.C. 4 is the true commencement of the Christian era, this date coincides remarkably with the number of the beast in the Apocalypse. In A.D. 663, Pope Vitalian enjoined the exclusive use of the Latin tongue in the offices of Divine worship throughout Christendom, and thus completed the development of the Latin or Roman Church. The two other thirds include the 42 months of his permitted power, and the time of the end, the 75 added days.

But the 666 and 1260 years which form the main part of this bi-millennial period, as well as the previous three and a half times, may be reckoned either in solar or lunar time. Now $666+1260$ solar years $= 666+1260+75$ lunar years. When the 75 lunar years were complete 75 more solar years might supervene. The threefold division $666+1260+75$ becomes in the latter case $666+1260+150$ years, or the third period of the time of the end would be doubled, and amount to five prophetic months. There is, first, the time before the rise of the beast; secondly, the time of his reign or predominance; thirdly, the time of the end, when his dominion has been taken away by the word and Spirit of God. Thus the nativity of the beast is approximately at the middle of the seventh century, and the time of the end, when his dominion is passing away, from the middle of the present or nineteenth century to the close of the next.

But the number of the beast has also a moral character. The three letters that compose it refer us expressly to two great events of the Old Testament history, Judg. xviii. 16, and Dan. iii. 1–12. The first of these shows in the history of the 600 Danites, the entrance and triumph of idolatry in Israel in its democratic form. The second, in the worship of the great image, of which the height was

sixty cubits and the breadth six cubits, is a striking
picture in the person of the great king and all his royal
counsellors, of an idolatrous monarch and an idolatrous
aristocracy. The three together form a trinal apostasy
of an idolatrous king, an idolatrous aristocracy, and an
idolatrous commonalty. The reference to the second
passage is explicit and clear in these words of the prophecy, " He had power to cause that whosoever would
not worship the image of the beast should be killed "
(chap. xiii. 15). The reference to the other passage, and
the history of the 600 Danites, though more indirect, is
not less striking. The tribe of Dan is the only tribe
omitted among the sealed tribes (ch. vii.; xiii. 18;
xix. 1).

This number of the beast seems to be still further a
key to the great system of prophetic times. It is two-
thirds of a millennium, and the four thousand years before
Christ form six such periods, and the two thousand years
after Christ three such periods. The millennium would
be one such period and a half, but is followed by " a little
season," making up a total of eleven great units, or seven
millennia and a third. The total excess of the world's
history over 7000 years, on this view, would be 336 years.
Now the excess in the first 6000 seems to be just half
this, 168 years, or four great millennial hours.

The Christian era according to Clinton, agreeing almost
exactly with the Pseudo-Enoch in the second century, is
B.C. 4136. A.D. 2032 is the close of the first Julian tetrad
when full 2000 years have been complete after the Ascension of Christ into heaven. The conjoint excess, 168
years, is four hours, or one sixth of a millennial day. A
like excess at the close of the millennium would complete
the whole to seven millennia and a third, or eleven times

the number of the beast, the same period already indicated at page 118.

VI. The *heads of the Beast.*

The passage on the heads of the beast (chap. xvii. 9–12) is another key to which the Holy Spirit directs our attention by a special note, " Here is the mind which hath wisdom." The interval between the time when the prophecy was given and the rise of the beast of chap. xiii. and xvii., or of the eighth and anti-christian head, is distinguished into three portions; the time of the five first heads and part of the sixth, was past already when the prophecy was given. There remained, first, the residue of the time of the then existent sixth head ; secondly, the time of the seventh head, of which it is said, " When he cometh he must exist a short space "; thirdly, a time of the non-existence or disappearance of the beast, before his re-appearance in a revived form. The interval from the date of the prophecy A.D. 96, to A.D. 666, is trisected in the years 286 and 476, and these are the eras of the reconstitution of the empire under Diocletian and Maximian, and of the fall of the last Western emperor, Augustulus. Thirty years after the date of the Prophecy, or A.D. 126, the tenth of Adrian, may be viewed as a climax, or height, of the then existing headship of Rome. From this date to A.D. 666, the technical date of the rise of the Neo-Latin kingdom is exactly a time and a half, 540 years. The first half-time reaches to A.D. 306, the accession of Constantine, in the midst of the great persecution (Rev. ii. 10). The sixth was by that time succeeded by the seventh or diademed headship of Diocletian and his successors. The change to a distinct headship is doubly marked, by the assumption of the diadem as an imperial *symbol,* and by the tetrapartite division of the empire under two Augusti and two Cæsars. This second stage, or the seventh head, lasted to the fall of the Western Empire under Augustulus, A.D. 476. To this head the description is given, "when he cometh he must continue a little space." The third stage is that of the *non esse*, or disappearance of the beast, in his character as a beast, till the rise of the Neo-Latin or Papal dominion. During this stage the Latin character of the dominion was suspended by the transfer of the seat of government from Rome to the East. The bestial character was also suspended, and a man's heart was given to it, by the acceptance of the Christian faith under Theodosius and his successors, before the time of the eighth or revived headship had fully come (Dan. vii. 4 ; v. 12, 29).

Thus the series of times separates itself into six divisions. 1. The time of the five fallen heads, and of the sixth head from the accession of Augustus, B.C. 27, to the date of the prophecy. 2. The residue of the sixth headship. 3. The seventh headship, to the fall of the Western Empire A.D. 476. 4. The stage when the beast "is not, and yet is," Rev. xvii. 8, or again xiii. 3, when one of the heads had been "wounded to death, before his wound is healed." A.D. 476 to 666. 5. The forty-two months (Rev. xiii. 5), or from A.D. 666 to 1926, (or 1850 by lunar reckoning), when "the deadly wound has been healed, and all the world wonders after the beast. 6. The "time of the end," or the "last days," of 2 Tim. iii. when the "latter times" of 1 Tim. iv. 1, have nearly run their course. The length of this last period seems to be from five to seven prophetic months of thirty years, and the first of these has already expired, so that only from 120 to 180 years of reprieve to the guilty nations and the visible Church remain. During this interval how earnestly should every true believer in God's holy word plead His promise of the "latter rain" of the Spirit (Joel ii. 23–32), till the time of long predicted judgment, the resurrection of the just, and the coming of those new heavens and that new earth, wherein righteousness shall dwell for ever; the accomplishment of the daily prayer of the Church, "Our Father which art in heaven, hallowed be Thy Name, Thy kingdom come; The will be done in earth as it is in heaven."

vii. The "Time," of Rev. x. 6.

The καιρὸς of Acts i. 7. 1 Thes. v. 1. 1 Tim. iv. 1. Rev. xii. 14. Dan. xii. 7. Rev. vi. 11. is a prophetic period of twelve prophetic months, or 360 solar years.

The χρόνος is not, as I once thought, the same period, but rather, as I now believe, a half millennium.

The six week-day millennia of the world's history may be regarded as making up one great working day of twelve hours, and the χρόνος or half millennium is one such hour. The angel lifting up his hands to heaven, and swearing that there shall be a time no longer, marks on the dial of time that the eleventh hour is ended, and the twelfth hour is come, the last before the sabbath eventide of rest.

The epoch of this oath answers in the fulfilment of the vision to the era of the Reformation, about A.D. 1520.

Now 360 years from A.D. 1520 bring us to 1880. But the oath is not that there shall no longer be a καιρός, but that there shall no longer be a χρόνος. The difference of terms indicates a difference in the period intended. From the Reformation, at the beginning of the 16th century, the limit of delay may be extended for one half millennium. It is not, however, to be supposed

that the oath defines the limit of delay so rigidly that no
latitude is allowed. The dates assigned to the birth of
Christ vary within a period of two Julian units, from
B.C. 8 to the ordinary Christian era, which happens to be
fixed in a leap year. The dates assignable to the angelic
oath vary from A.D. 1516 to 1524. These two tetrads include the great climax of the Reformation, and nearly all
the critical changes of it. A third of 1524 years is 508
years. Taking a Julian unit of four years instead of a
prophetic month of 30 years, as the latitude or limit of
error purposely left in the definition of the period specified
as a χρόνος, we may remark that if a millennium were
reckoned at 2^{10} or 1024 years, a half millennium would
be 2^9 or 512 years, or 128 Julian units.

Each χρόνος or half millennium will of course contain
12 hours of a whole millennial νυχθήμερον or week-day,
and the hour of a millennial week-day will be 42 Julian
years, as 42 is the nearest integer to $\frac{1000}{24}$, so a χρόνος will
be at least 12 x 42 or 504 years, and a bare period of five
centuries is at least a Julian unit in defect.

Again, if a millennium be reckoned at 1020 years, a
χρόνος, or half millennium will be 510 years, or, a
prophetic καιρὸς of 360 years + 5 prophetic or year-day
months, making 17 prophetic months in all.

Eight Julian units in excess of the year 2000 of the
common era, will complete two such millennia from
B.C. 8, the limit of the earliest date assignable for the
actual birth of Christ.

The χρόνος might be 504, 508, 510, or 512 years.

What then will be the import of the solemn oath of
the angel, Rev. x. 6 ? That a χρόνος, or one-fourth of
the prophetical 2000 years after the Messiah, will not
be complete from the date of that oath (the Protestant

Reformation, A.D. 1516) to the time of the last Trumpet and the close of the mystery of Providence. The days may be "shortened," but are not to be prolonged beyond this interval, or probably, A.D. 2030.

Of this half millennial day, these twelve millennial hours of reprieve and Divine long-suffering implied in that oath, seven had elapsed in 1814, or at the date of the European peace and the triumph of our country sixty years ago. During those three centuries, by the blessing of God, our country was maintained on the rock of a public covenant with God, of faith in the Bible and Christianity, and of a national protest against the mystic Babylon.

During the last half century, under the conjoint influence of the Tractarian conspiracy to undo the work of the Reformation, and of the pseudo-liberal statesmanship which ceases alike to hold fast the national faith in Christ and the everlasting Gospel, and to protest against the Church of Rome, our country has been drifting away from the rock on which it was planted by the faith and zeal of our reformers 300 years ago.

There are still probably from four to six prophetic months remaining, from 120 to 180 years, in which the downward course may yet be reversed, and, by the blessing of God, our great empire might resume its high calling as the chief witness for God and His truth in the last days, and be rescued from a gulf of solemn and fearful judgment, towards which pilots in Church and State, as blind as they are boastful, in the name of progress, have been steadily steering.

The whole course of the world's history, it would result from the above remarks, consists of seven and a third millennia.

We have now, in the year of the world 6026, reached

that stage of the great scheme of Providence, when the six completed week-days are passed, and there remains only a millennial sabbath, with the added third of a millennium shared between a season of the filling up of the Divine long-suffering which is its preface, and the " little season " of a permitted renewal of temptation and sin at its close.

The few years of the 61st century already past have been marked by four great events. The decree of the Vatican Council completing and crowning the Western Apostasy ; the war of France and Prussia, involving the overthrow of the Napoleonic dynasty; the war of Russia and Turkey, followed by the further dismemberment of the latter, and the fresh defeat of the ambition of the great king of the North ; and the recent General Election in England, in which it seems as if the first of Protestant powers were ready to renounce its national faith in God and in Christ, and to resolve itself, in the name of liberty, into a chaos of unbelieving atoms. Attempts at regicide in the European kingdoms are so frequent that the very foundations are destroyed, and the most atrocious blasphemies against God are so prevalent that even Christians cease to be shocked when they hear them. The holiness and the truth of God both require that His judgments should be fulfilled in their due season. But the foul and multiplied reproaches, the " hard speeches which ungodly sinners have spoken against Him," because of those very threatenings, as if the God of Love were a Moloch of cruelty, make it essential for the vindication of His great name, that His long-suffering towards human wickedness should outlast and exceed the patience of the best and kindest of men. " When the Son of man cometh shall He find faith on the earth ? " God's own patience must

K

continue till His servants are ready to complain that He
has forgotten His promise. In a much earlier stage of
God's providence, the faith first of David (Ps. lxxiii), and
next of Jeremiah (Jer. xii.), was ready to fail in the
presence of wickedness prosperous and still unpunished.
St. Peter gives us the key to this mystery of grace, in
closest connection with the Divine calendar of the "times."
"Beloved, be not ignorant of this one thing, that one day
is with the Lord as a thousand years, and a thousand years
as one day. The Lord is not slack concerning His
promise as some men count it slackness, but is long-
suffering to usward, not willing that any should perish,
but that all should come to repentance."

To have an intense longing desire for the return of
Christ and the promised resurrection of the just, because
of the greatness of the blessings then to follow and of
the evils then to be terminated; but also an intense
sympathy with the patience of God and the long-suffering
of Christ; these are the two pivots of grace and righteousness on which the soul of the Christian must revolve.
Those whose duty it is to be "Epistles of Christ" should
reflect and image to the world the glorious perfections
of their Heavenly Father.

CPSIA information can be obtained
at www.ICGtesting.com
Printed in the USA
BVHW040947240820
587131BV00018B/501

9 781165 143054